GO FOR IT, MARIA-CHAN! PROPER USE OF A ROD

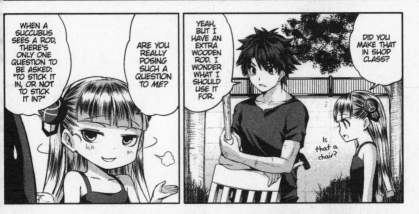

WHEN A SUCCUBUS SEES A ROD, THERE'S ONLY ONE QUESTION TO BE ASKED: "TO STICK IT IN, OR NOT TO STICK IT IN?"

ARE YOU REALLY POSING SUCH A QUESTION TO ME?

YEAH, BUT I HAVE AN EXTRA WOODEN ROD. I WONDER WHAT I SHOULD USE IT FOR.

DID YOU MAKE THAT IN SHOP CLASS?

Is that a chair?

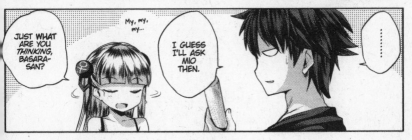

JUST WHAT ARE YOU THINKING, BASARA-SAN?

My, my, my...

I GUESS I'LL ASK MIO THEN.

....

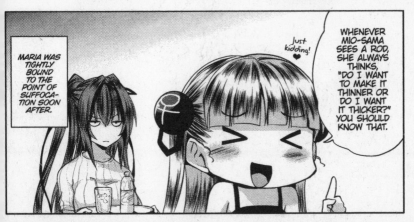

MARIA WAS TIGHTLY BOUND TO THE POINT OF SUFFOCATION SOON AFTER.

Just kidding!

WHENEVER MIO-SAMA SEES A ROD, SHE ALWAYS THINKS, "DO I WANT TO MAKE IT THINNER OR DO I WANT IT THICKER?" YOU SHOULD KNOW THAT.

AFTERWORD 6

Thanks so much everyone for buying *The Testament of Sister New Devil* volume 6. As you have come to know by now, I am Miyakokasiwa.

So, this manga version has finally gotten to the **Zolgia** arc. I'm sure there are many people out there who have already seen this in the anime or read it in the novels, but I'm rolling up my sleeves a bit in an attempt to expand or develop things in a way to keep you on your toes. On second thought...it's a little too cold for that, so I'll pull them back down and just give it everything I've got! With that little pep talk, I hope you all do look forward to what's to come.

The anime has gotten a second season and there's even been a spin off novel coming out (the illustrations and supervision of which I have been put in charge of) and so the world of *Sister New Devil* has grown, and on that note, I hope to increase the tension in the manga--so I hope you will all keep following it.

Wow... I was actually somewhat serious this time! I'll just have to kid around and goof off more in volume 7! See you then!

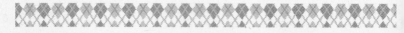

STAFF

tetsu
色s
亀井希弥
8股のおろち
天野かすた
つくしろ夕莉
けう
樋上

THANKS

上栖先生　大熊先生
戸堀さん　森丘さん
大輝さん　岸田さん
梶本さん　笹尾さん

2015.7

The Testament of
Sister New Devil

Bring me some tea!

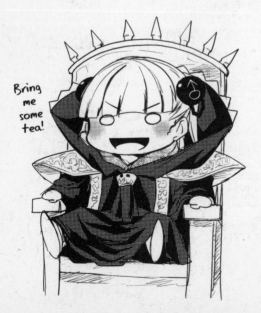

"I'LL CRUSH YOU RIGHT HERE... JUST KIDDING."

SHIBA KYOUICHI

COMBAT STYLE

????????

A guy who smiles way too much, with an adamant and aloof air about him. However, his power is so great that he frightens Takashi, and just going up against him makes Basara extremely nervous. Surely some vast power lies hidden within him.

COMBAT PARAMETERS

POWER — ?

SPEED — ?

SKILL — ?

MANA — ?

POWER

SKILL — ? — SPEED

MANA

EQUIPMENT ????

Even without a weapon, he has the incredible ability to break down an erect magical barrier with his bare hands.

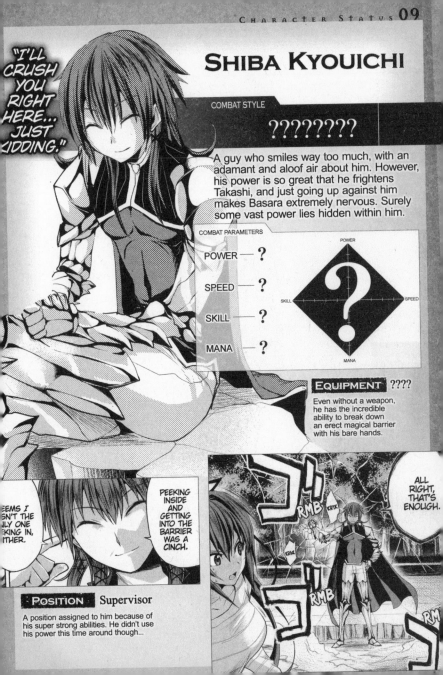

EEMS I SN'T THE LY ONE EKING IN, THER.

PEEKING INSIDE AND GETTING INTO THE BARRIER WAS A CINCH.

ALL RIGHT, THAT'S ENOUGH.

POSITION   Supervisor

A position assigned to him because of his super strong abilities. He didn't use his power this time around though...

NONAKA KURUMI

COMBAT STYLE

ELEMENTAL MASTER

MANA

"I'LL MAKE YOU REGRET EVERYTHING... WHAT YOU DID NOW AND BACK THEN!"

A master in the all-purpose Elemental Spirit magics, she can use limitless mana to bombard her opponents with a barrage of elemental magic.

COMBAT PARAMETERS

POWER — **D**

SPEED — **B**

SKILL — **B**

MANA — **A**

POWER

SKILL

SPEED

MANA

EQUIPMENT

THE GAUNTLETS OF THE ELEMENTALIST

Armaments which allow the user to open a channel to the elemental spirits. They increase the user's effectiveness by using elemental magic.

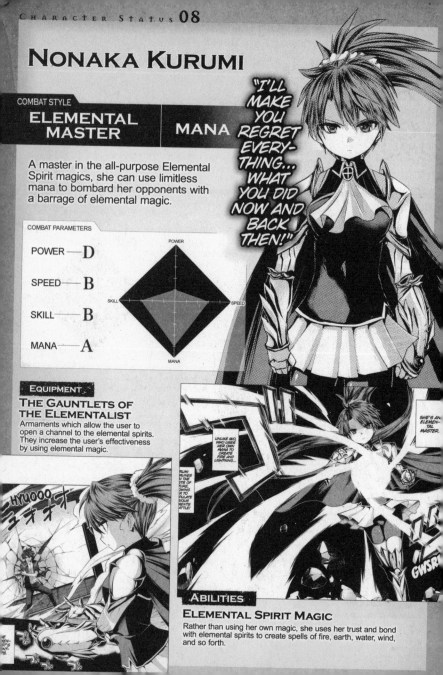

HYUOOOO
ユキオォォ

SHE'S AN ELEMENTAL MASTER.

UNLIKE IMO, WHO USES HER OWN MANA TO CREATE FIRE AND LIGHTNING...

KURUMI ATTUNES TO THE SPIRITS OF TERRA, USING RA TO MANIPULATE VARIOUS ELEMENTS TO HER ADVANTAGE.

GWSRI

ABILITIES

ELEMENTAL SPIRIT MAGIC

Rather than using her own magic, she uses her trust and bond with elemental spirits to create spells of fire, earth, water, wind, and so forth.

HAYASE TAKASHI

"RIP THEM TO SHREDS, BYAKKO!"

COMBAT STYLE

QUICK LANCER | SPEED

A spear wielder who uses extraordinary speed to disorient his foes while looking for an opening to take them down with a finishing blow. With the Divine Spear, "Byakko," his defense is greatly heightened and he has the power to unleash devastating wind attacks.

COMBAT PARAMETERS

POWER — C

SPEED — S

SKILL — A

MANA — C

POWER

SKILL

SPEED

MANA

EQUIPMENT

BYAKKO

A spear that houses the Divine Guardian Beast Byakko. It is capable of unleashing powerful wind-based attacks capable of rending its foes. However, it is limited by its creed to "protect the west" and should its user fail to do so, it will not be able to unleash its power.

HE GOT IN...!!

THR-CLANG

GWOOO

ABILITIES

With Byakko's ability to detect where its opponents are attacking from, Takashi is able to become a steel wall using his speed and skill to deflect his opponents' attacks.

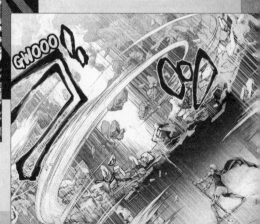

The Testament of
Sister New Devil

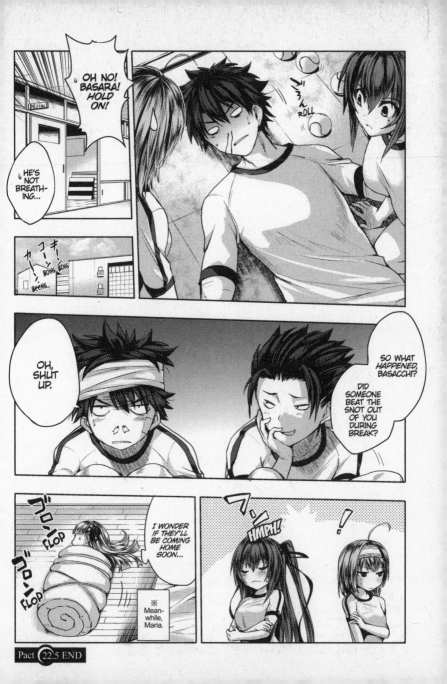

OH NO! BASARA! HOLD ON!

HE'S NOT BREATH-ING...

ロール ROLL

カ コーン キーン
BONG BING
BEENG

OH, SHUT UP.

SO WHAT HAPPENED, BASACCHI?

DID SOMEONE BEAT THE SNOT OUT OF YOU DURING BREAK?

FLOP FLOP FLOP

I WONDER IF THEY'LL BE COMING HOME SOON...

※ Mean-while, Maria.

HMPH!

!

Pact 22.5 END

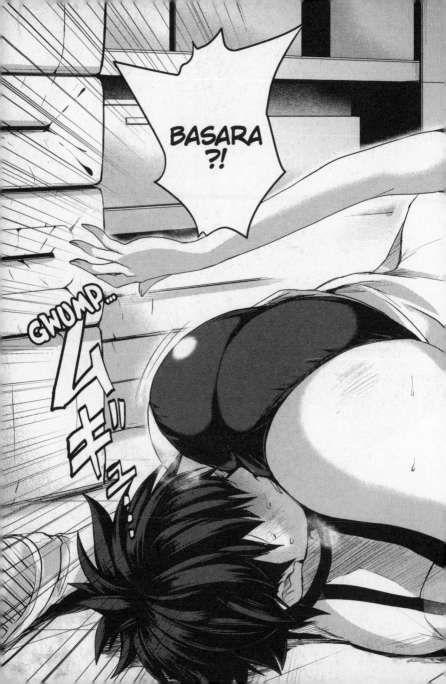

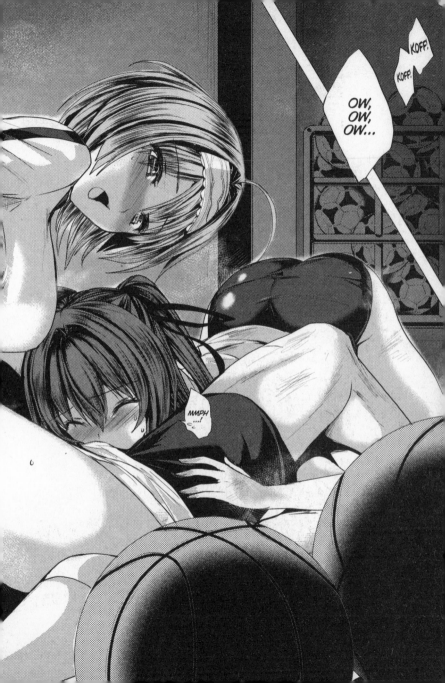

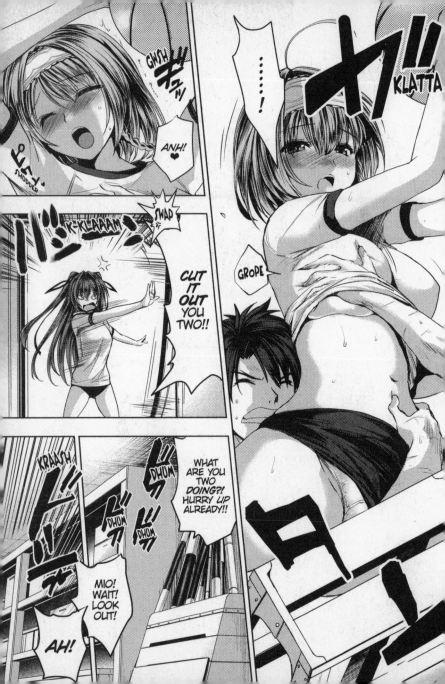

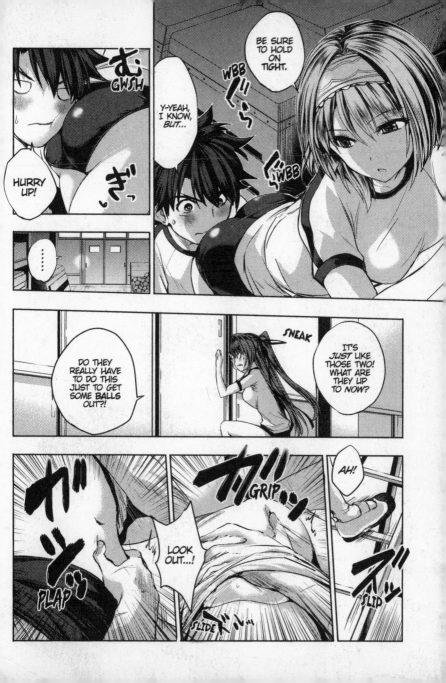

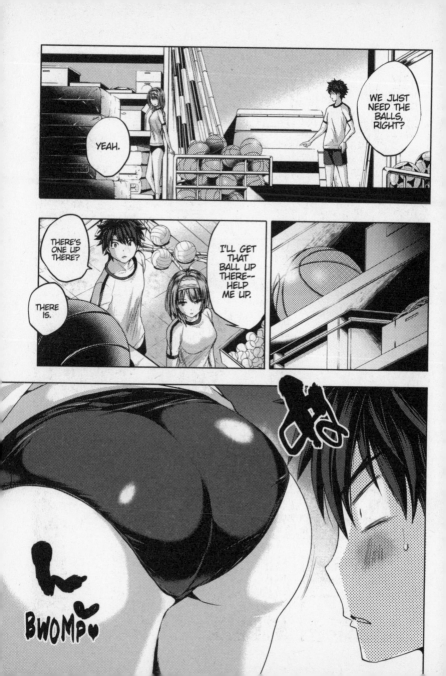

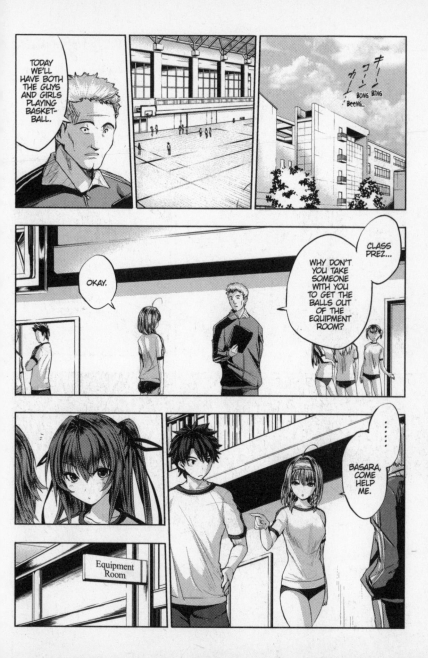

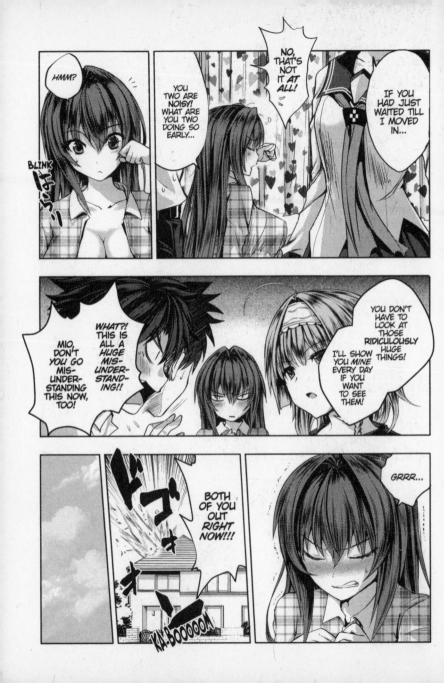

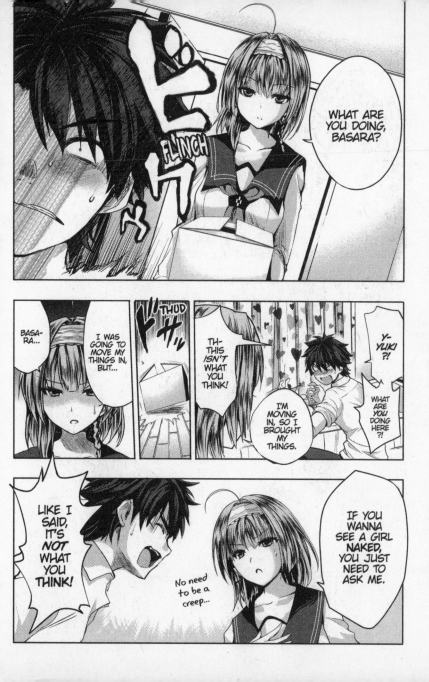

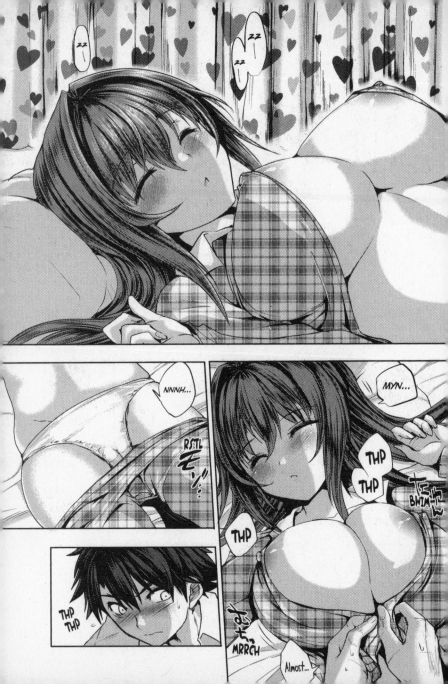

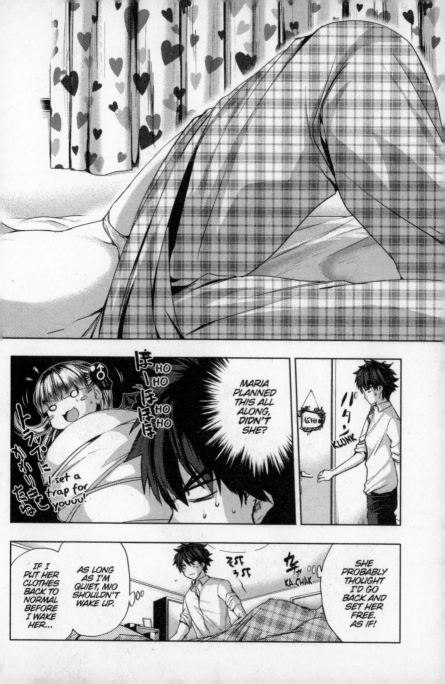

HO HO

HO HO

MARIA PLANNED THIS ALL ALONG, DIDN'T SHE?

KLUNK

I set a trap for youuu!

IF I PUT HER CLOTHES BACK TO NORMAL BEFORE I WAKE HER...

AS LONG AS I'M QUIET, MIO SHOULDN'T WAKE UP.

KA-CHAK

SHE PROBABLY THOUGHT I'D GO BACK AND SET HER FREE. AS IF!

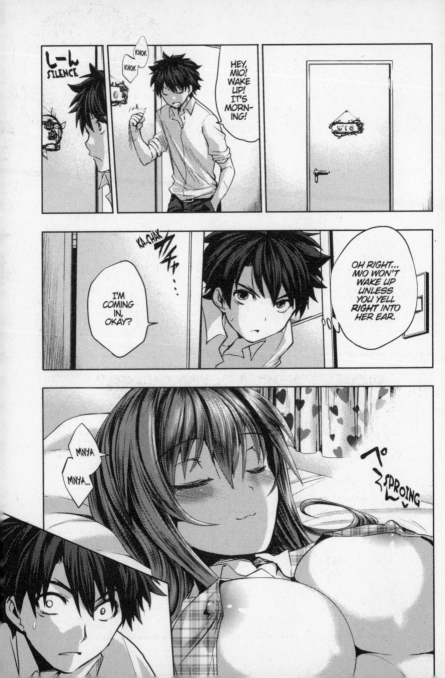

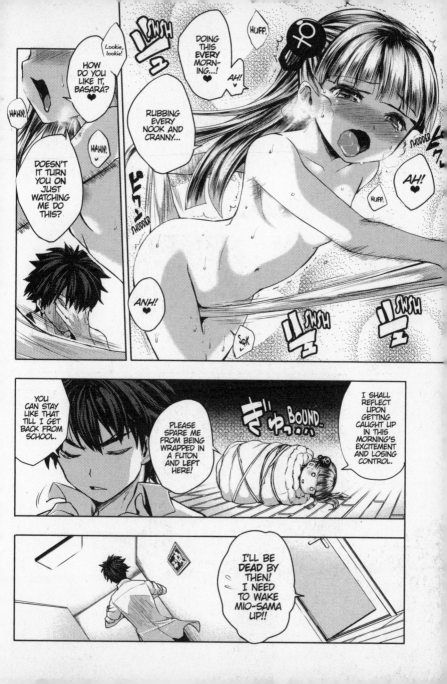

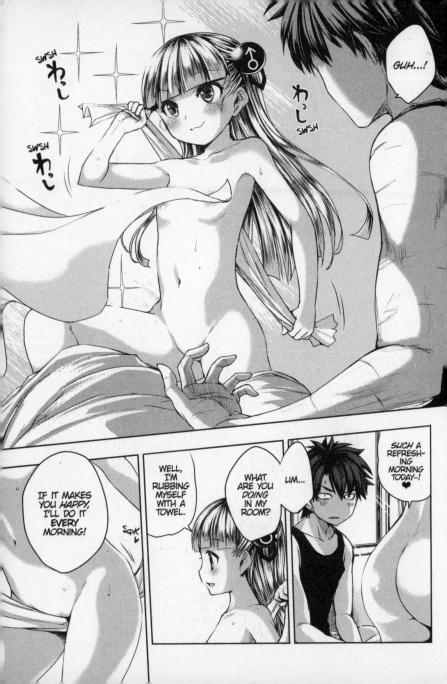

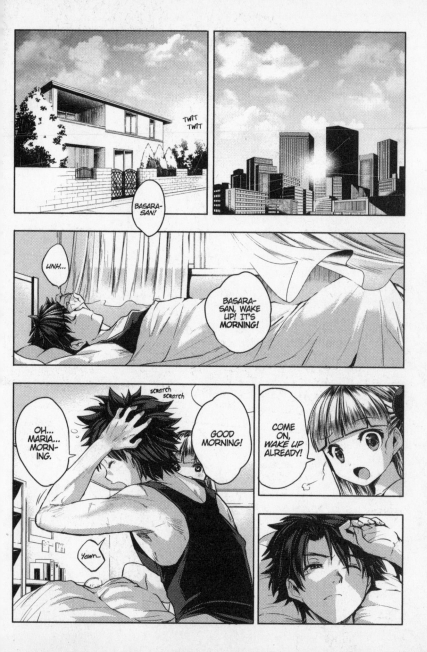

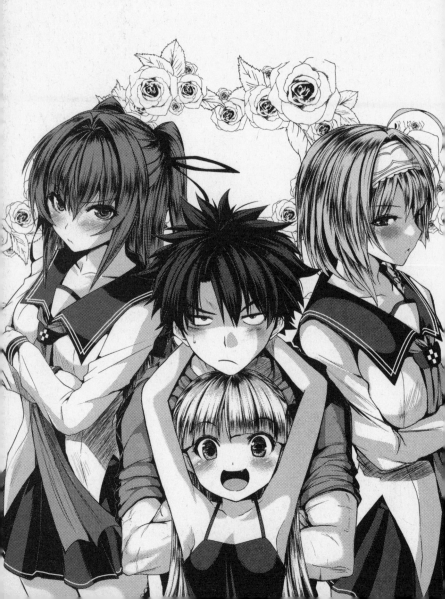

The Testament of
Sister New Devil

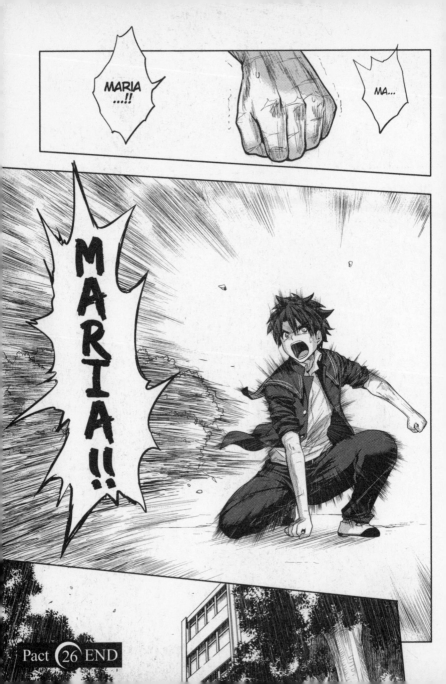

Pact 26 END

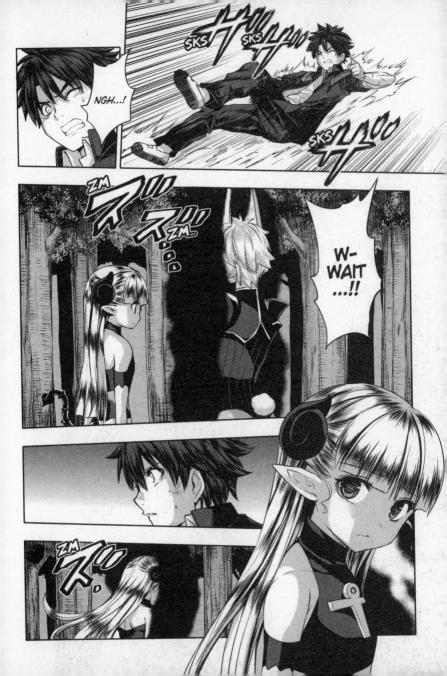

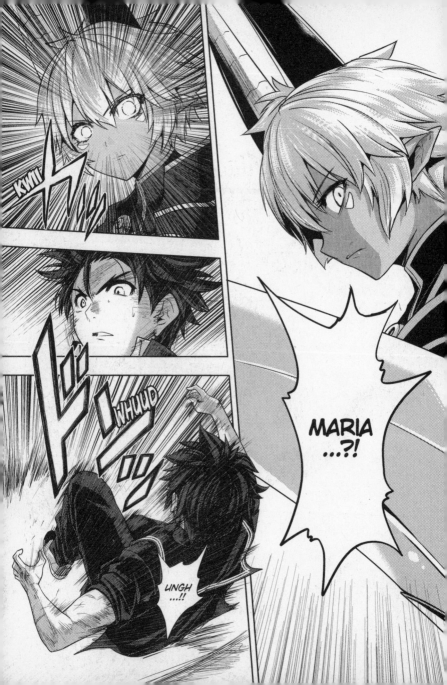

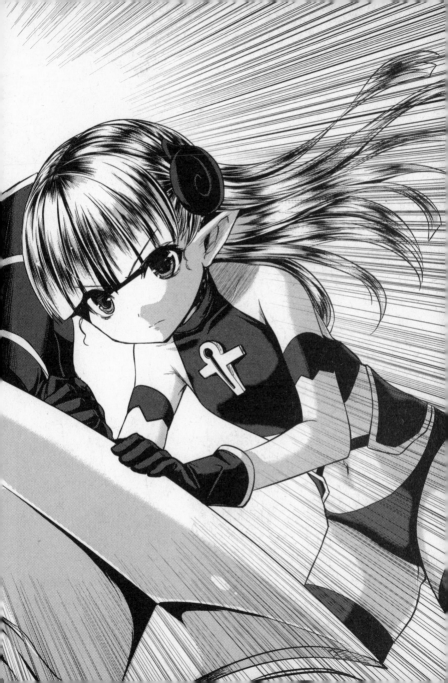

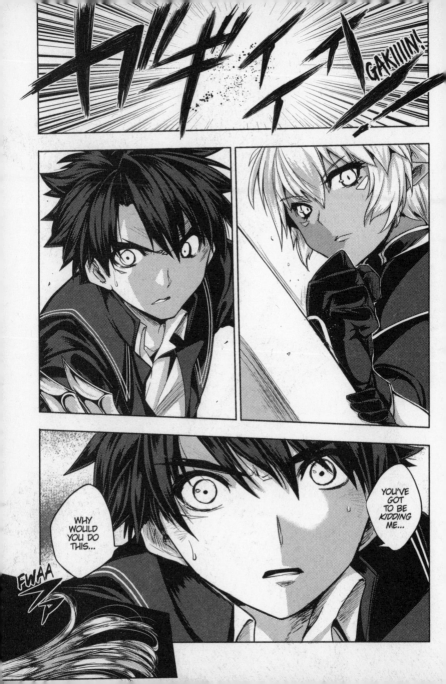

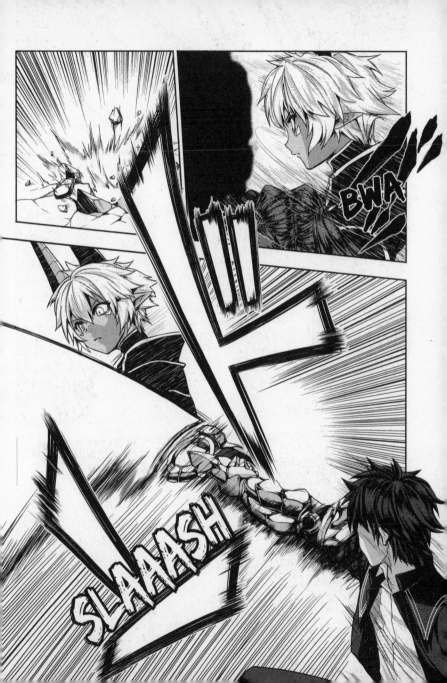

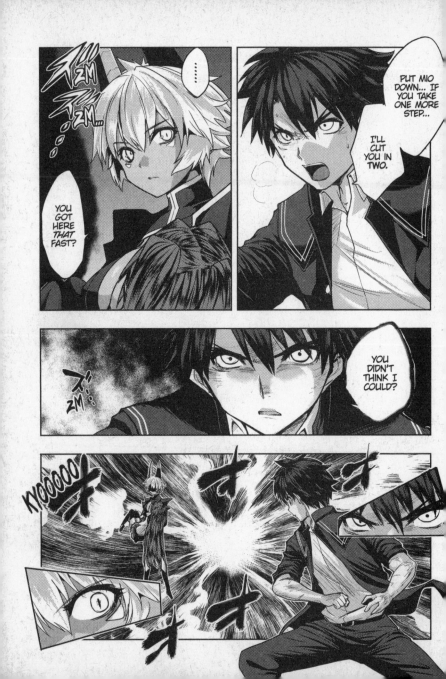

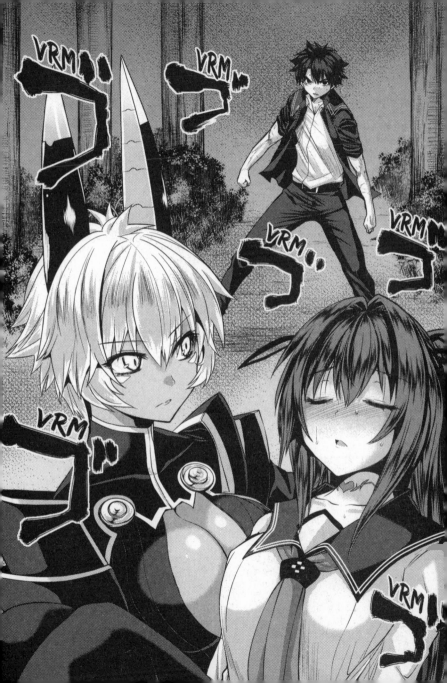

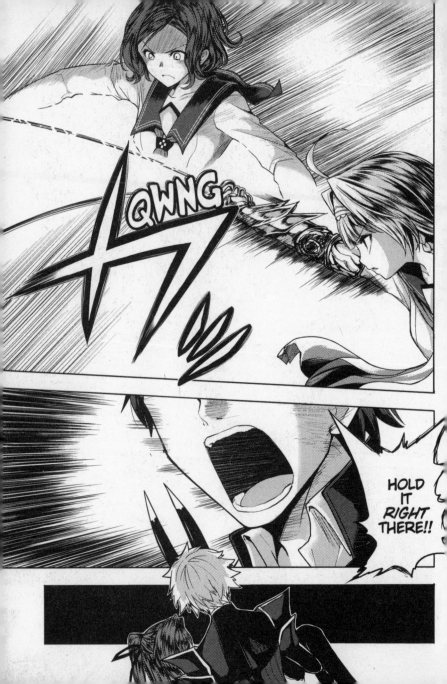

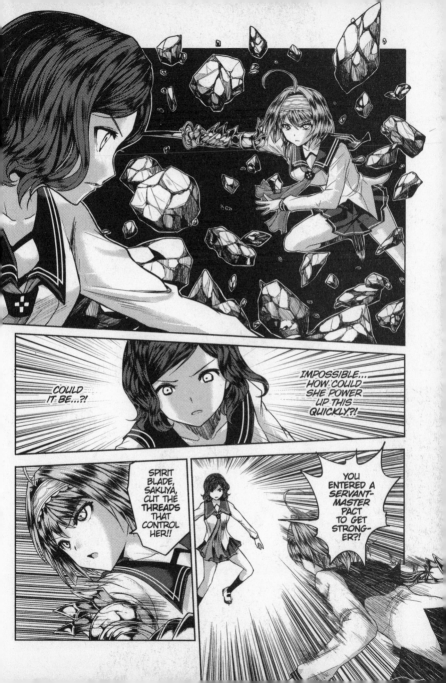

COULD IT BE...?!

IMPOSSIBLE... HOW COULD SHE POWER UP THIS QUICKLY?!

SPIRIT BLADE, SAKUYA, CUT THE THREADS THAT CONTROL HER!!

YOU ENTERED A SERVANT-MASTER PACT TO GET STRONGER?!

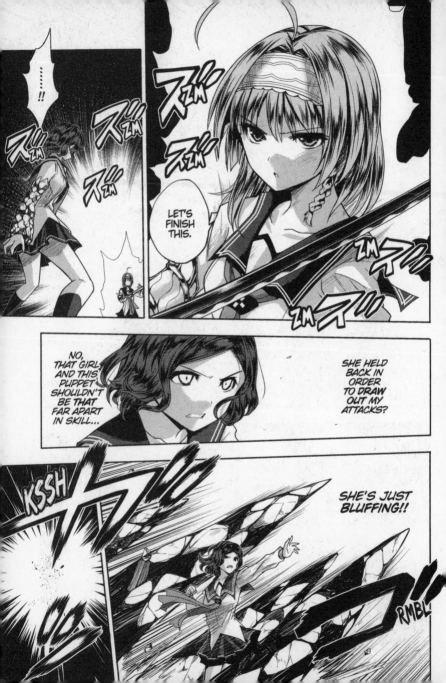

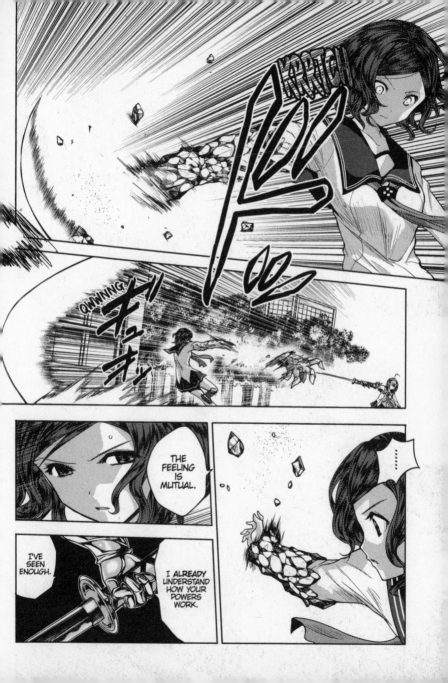

THE FEELING IS MUTUAL.

I'VE SEEN ENOUGH.

I ALREADY UNDERSTAND HOW YOUR POWERS WORK.

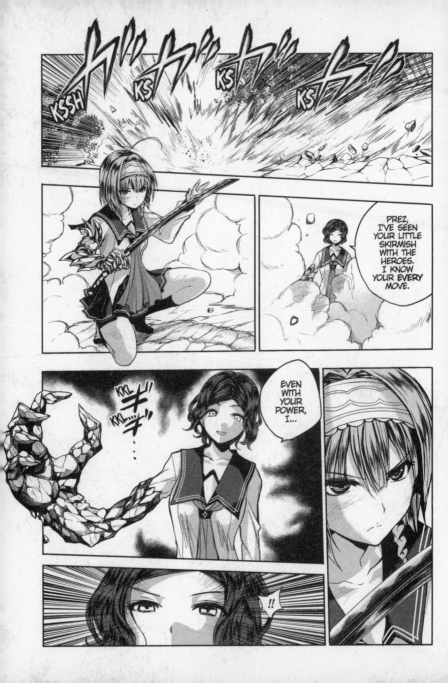

PREZ, I'VE SEEN YOUR LITTLE SKIRMISH WITH THE HEROES. I KNOW YOUR EVERY MOVE.

EVEN WITH YOUR POWER, I...

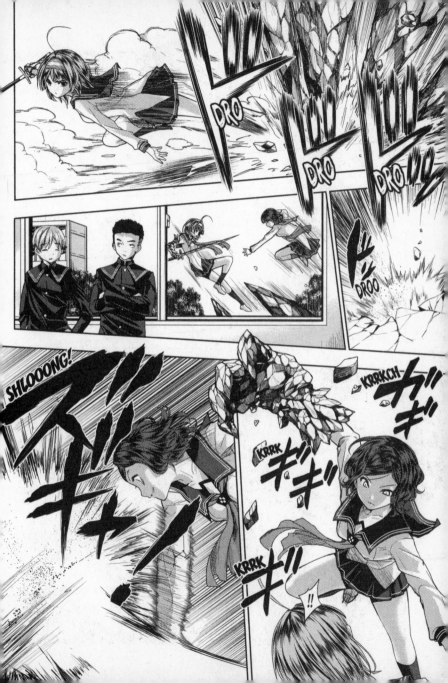

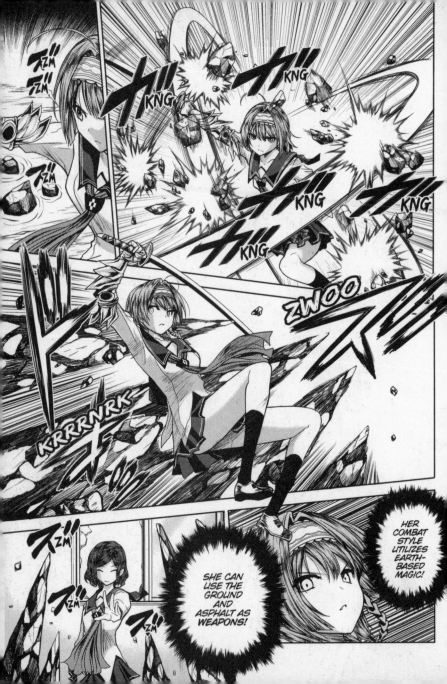

SHE CAN USE THE GROUND AND ASPHALT AS WEAPONS!

HER COMBAT STYLE UTILIZES EARTH-BASED MAGIC!

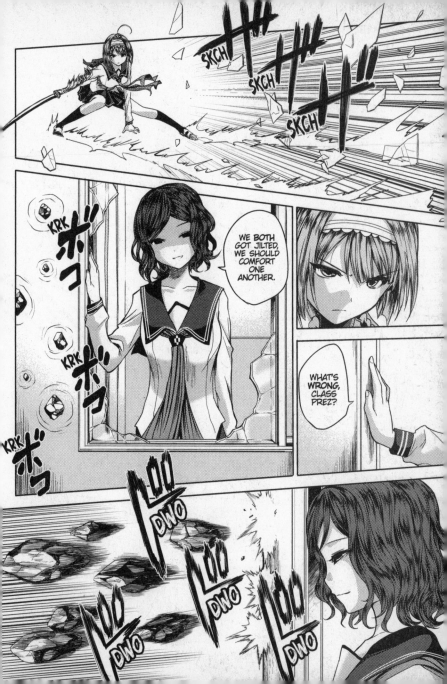

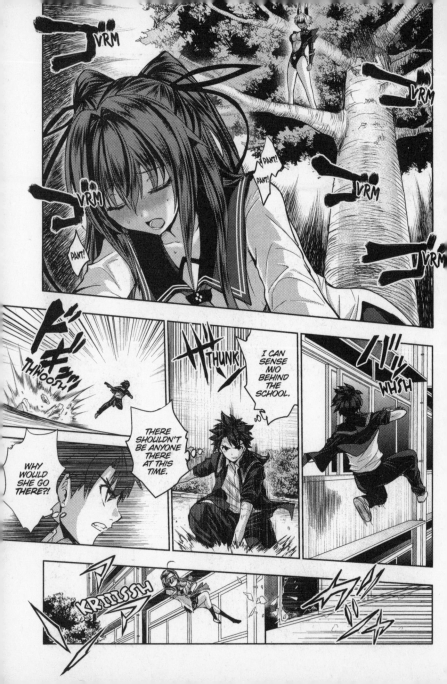

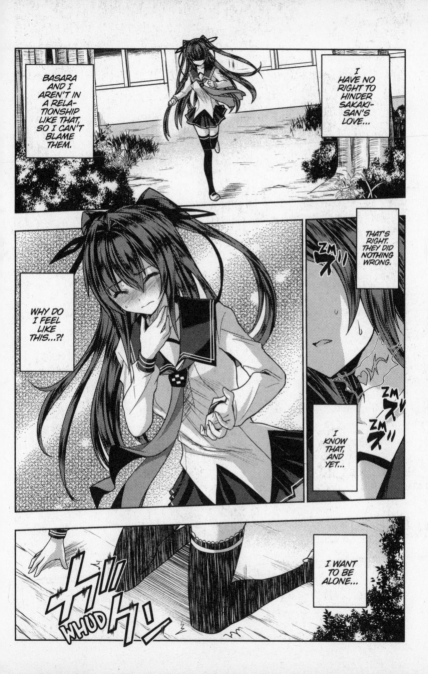

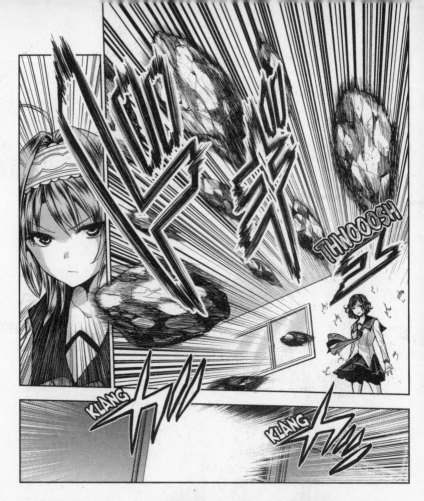

THWOOOSH

KLANG

KLANG

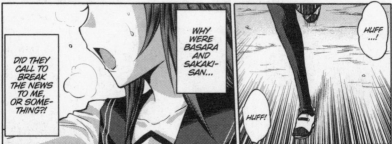

DID THEY CALL TO BREAK THE NEWS TO ME, OR SOME-THING?!

WHY WERE BASARA AND SAKAKI-SAN...

HUFF ....!

HUFF!

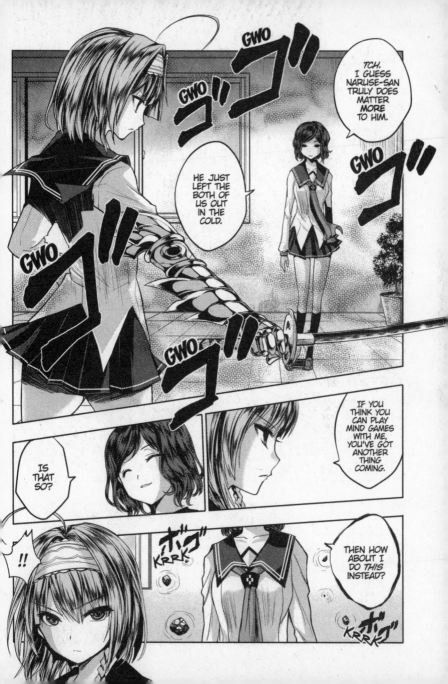

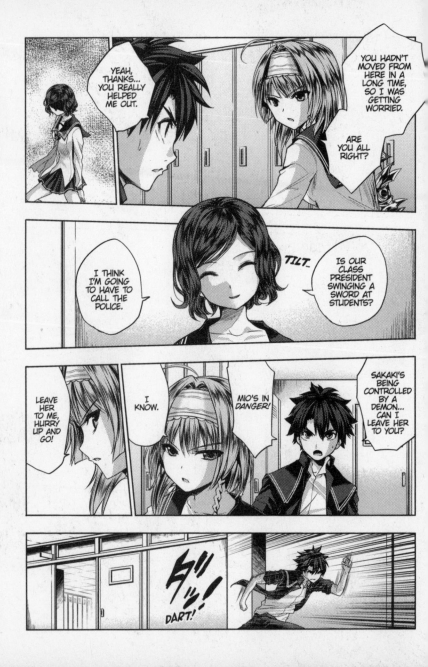

YEAH, THANKS... YOU REALLY HELPED ME OUT.

YOU HADN'T MOVED FROM HERE IN A LONG TIME, SO I WAS GETTING WORRIED.

ARE YOU ALL RIGHT?

TILT

I THINK I'M GOING TO HAVE TO CALL THE POLICE.

IS OUR CLASS PRESIDENT SWINGING A SWORD AT STUDENTS?

LEAVE HER TO ME, HURRY UP AND GO!

I KNOW.

MIO'S IN DANGER!

SAKAKI'S BEING CONTROLLED BY A DEMON... CAN I LEAVE HER TO YOU?

ダッ!!
DART!

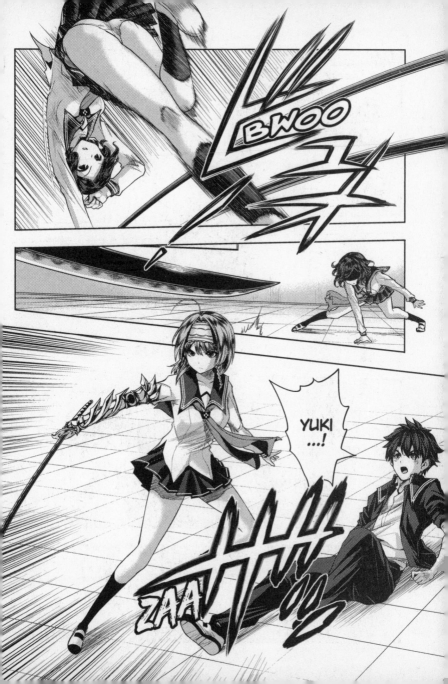

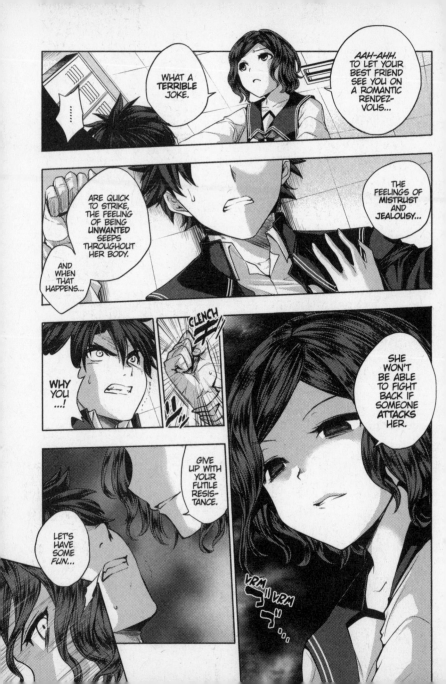

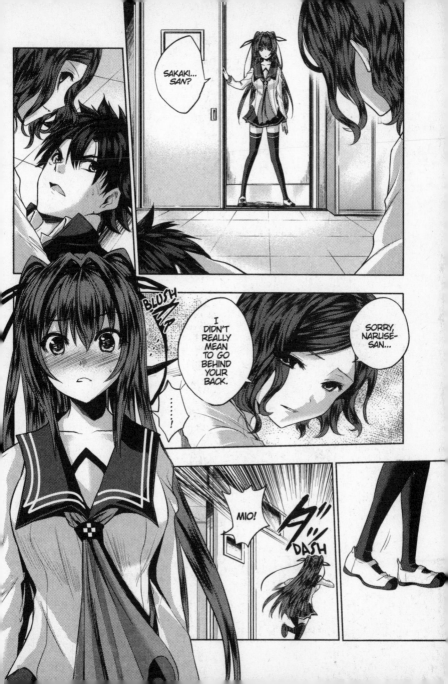

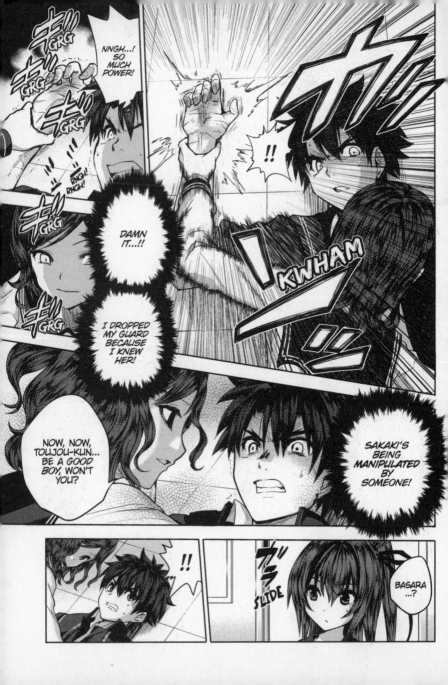

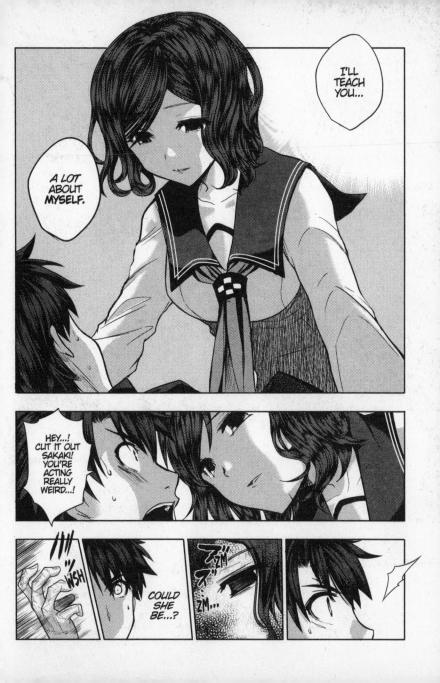

BOY'S LOCKER ROOM

THAT MEANS I STILL HAVE A CHANCE, RIGHT?

TH-WHUD

?!

TRIP

?!

HAVEN'T YOU NOTICED... HOW I FEEL?

HUH?

WHAT ?!

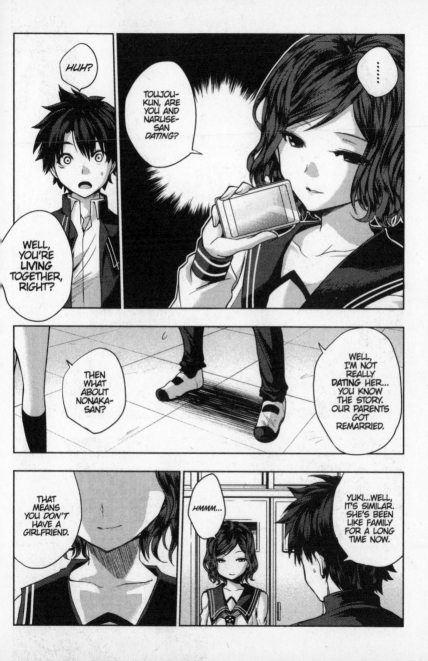

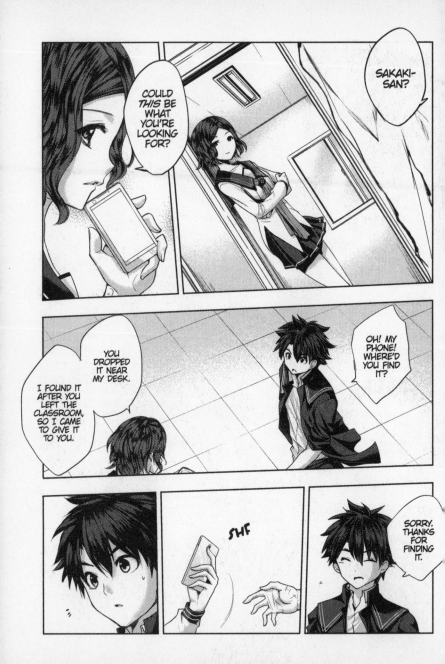

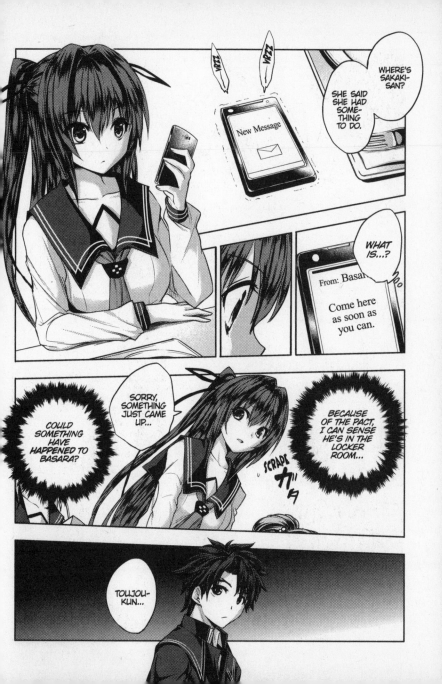

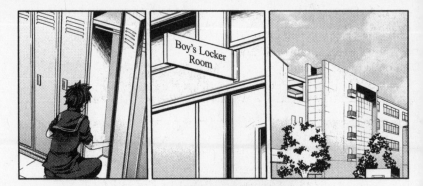

Boy's Locker Room

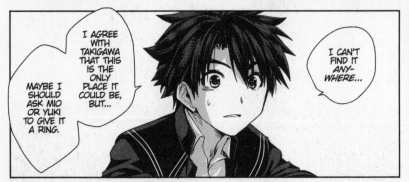

I AGREE WITH TAKIGAWA THAT THIS IS THE ONLY PLACE IT COULD BE, BUT...

MAYBE I SHOULD ASK MIO OR YUKI TO GIVE IT A RING.

I CAN'T FIND IT ANY-WHERE...

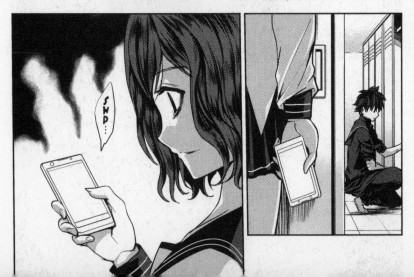

SWP...

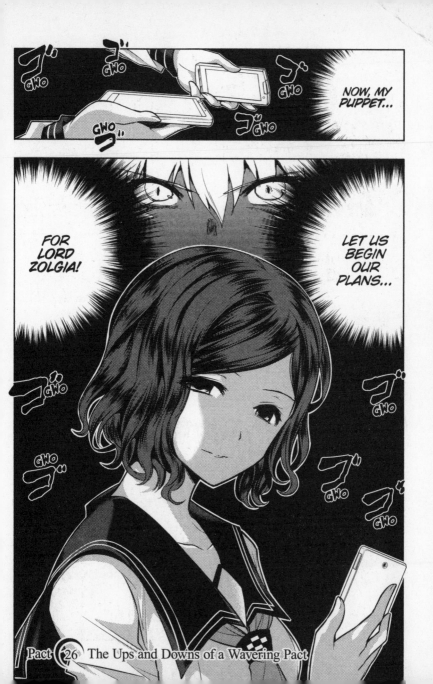

Pact 26 The Ups and Downs of a Wavering Pact

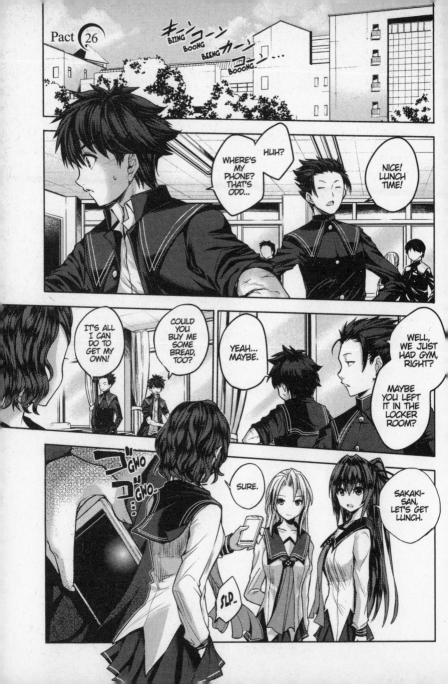

The Testament of
Sister New Devil

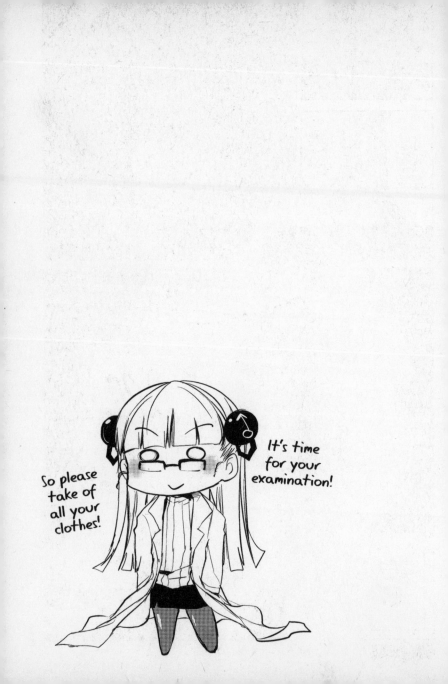

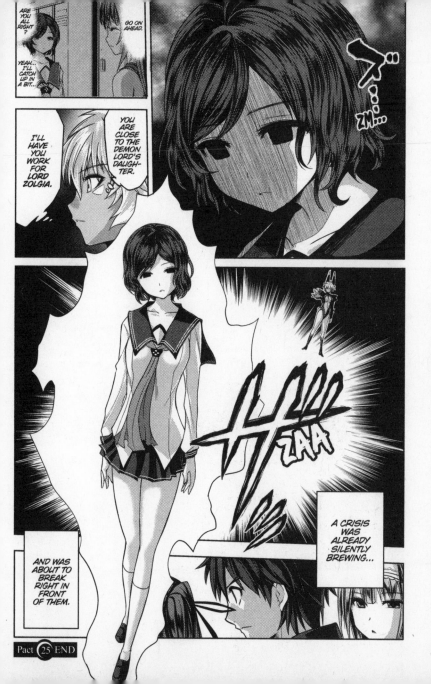

ARE YOU ALL RIGHT?

GO ON AHEAD.

YEAH... I'LL CATCH UP IN A BIT...

I'LL HAVE YOU WORK FOR LORD ZOLGIA.

YOU ARE CLOSE TO THE DEMON LORD'S DAUGHTER.

ZM...

HZAA

A CRISIS WAS ALREADY SILENTLY BREWING...

AND WAS ABOUT TO BREAK RIGHT IN FRONT OF THEM.

Pact 25 END

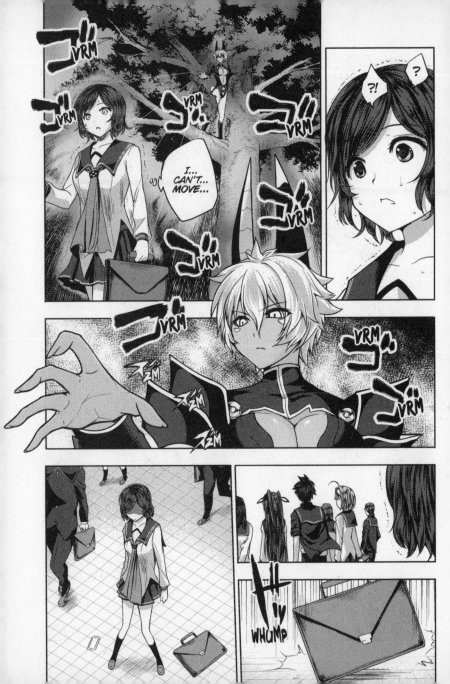

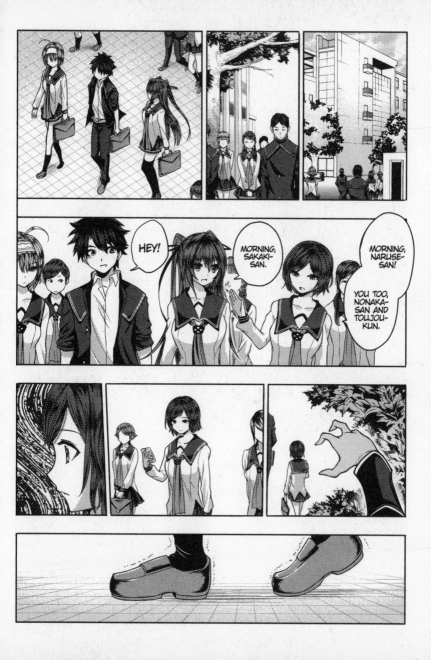

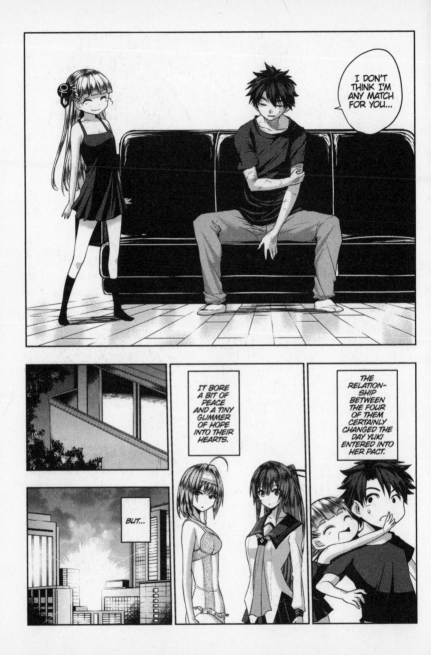

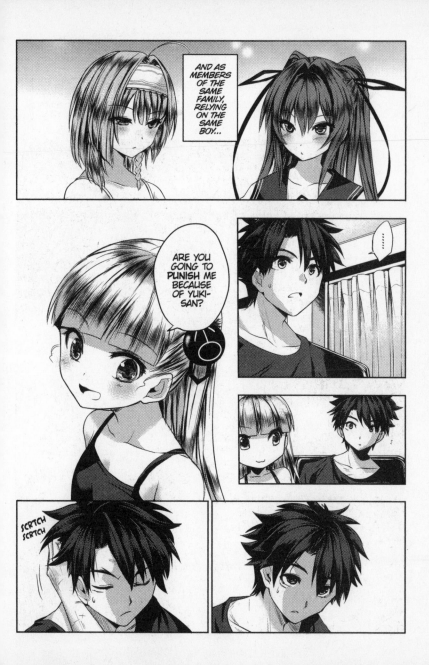

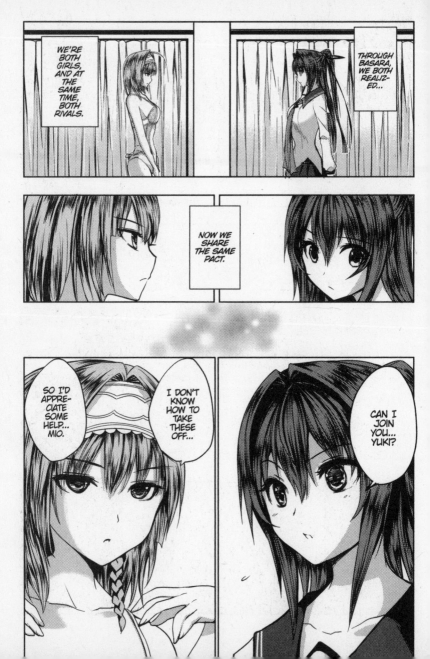

WE'RE BOTH GIRLS, AND AT THE SAME TIME, BOTH RIVALS.

THROUGH BASARA, WE BOTH REALIZED...

NOW WE SHARE THE SAME PACT.

SO I'D APPRECIATE SOME HELP... MIO.

I DON'T KNOW HOW TO TAKE THESE OFF...

CAN I JOIN YOU... YUKI?

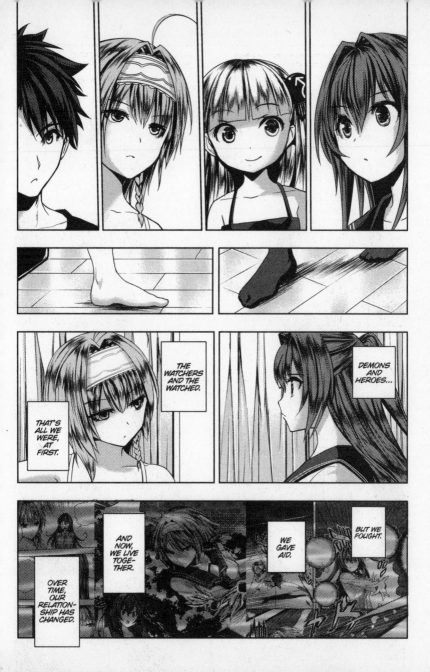

THE WATCHERS AND THE WATCHED.

THAT'S ALL WE WERE, AT FIRST.

DEMONS AND HEROES...

AND NOW, WE LIVE TOGETHER.

WE GAVE AID.

BUT WE FOUGHT.

OVER TIME, OUR RELATIONSHIP HAS CHANGED.

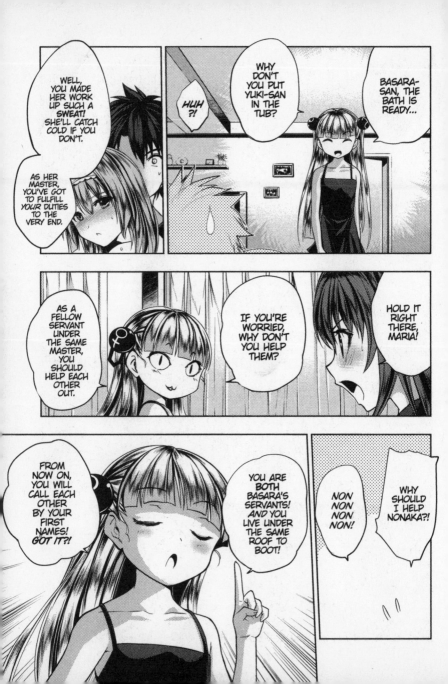

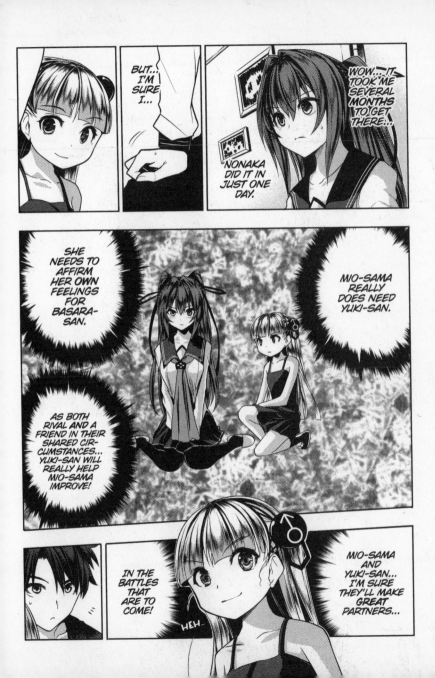

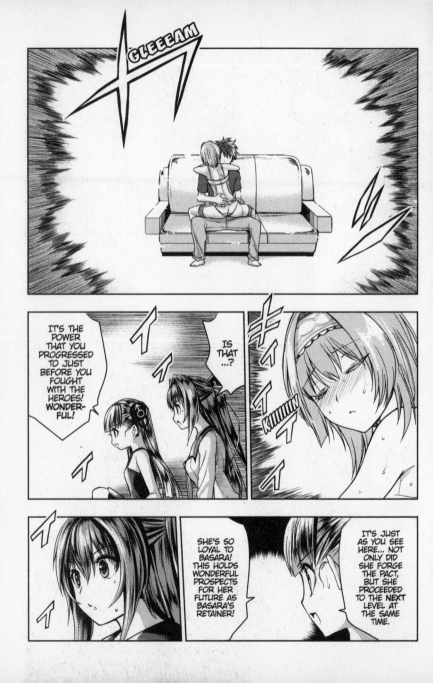

GLEEEAM

IT'S THE POWER THAT YOU PROGRESSED TO JUST BEFORE YOU FOUGHT WITH THE HEROES! WONDERFUL!

IS THAT...?

KIIIIIIN

SHE'S SO LOYAL TO BASARA! THIS HOLDS WONDERFUL PROSPECTS FOR HER FUTURE AS BASARA'S RETAINER!

IT'S JUST AS YOU SEE HERE... NOT ONLY DID SHE FORGE THE PACT, BUT SHE PROCEEDED TO THE NEXT LEVEL AT THE SAME TIME.

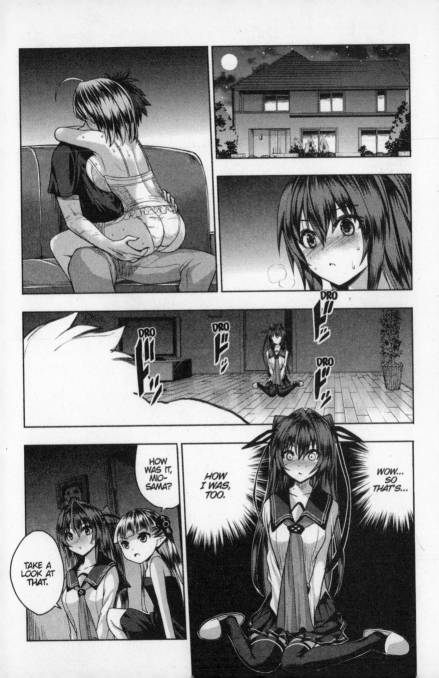

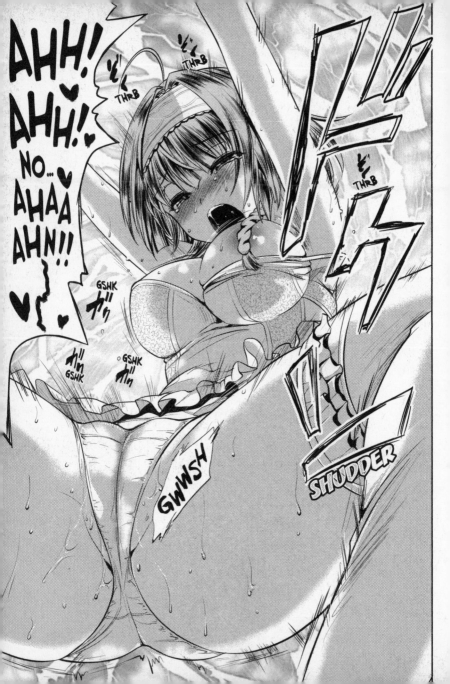

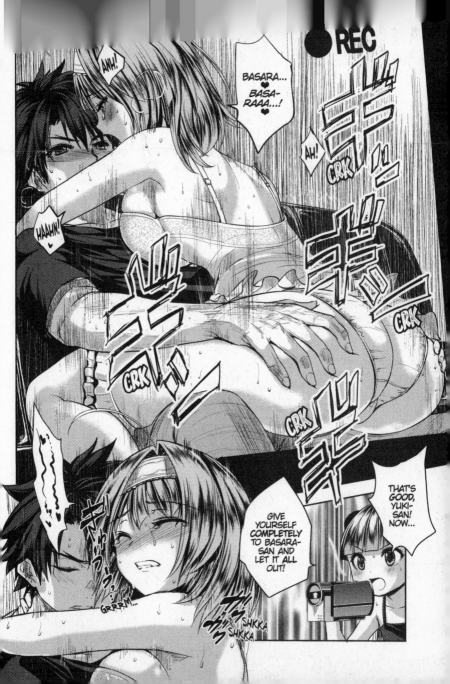

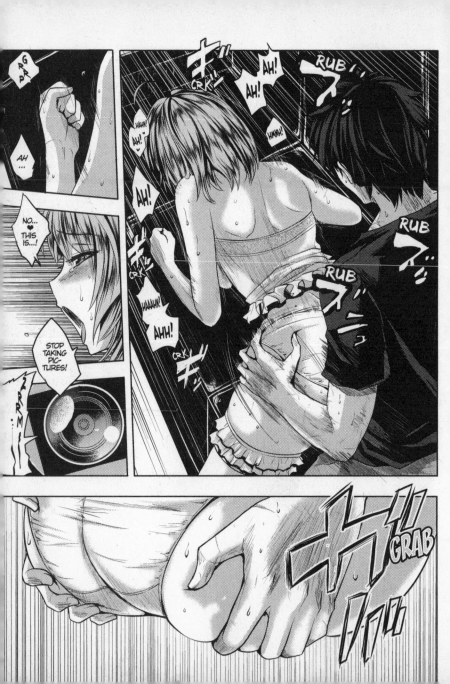

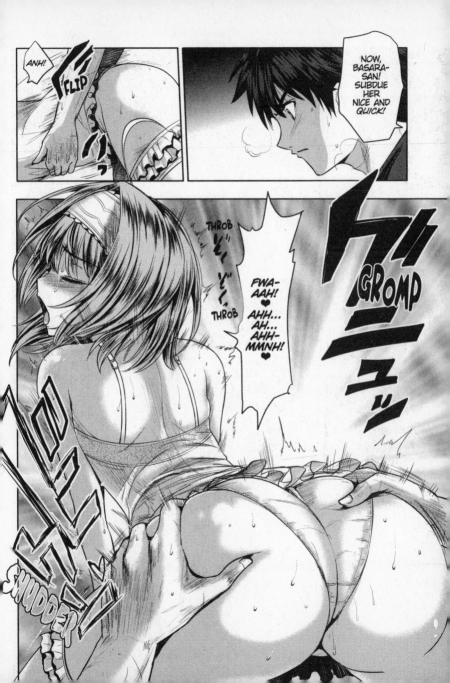

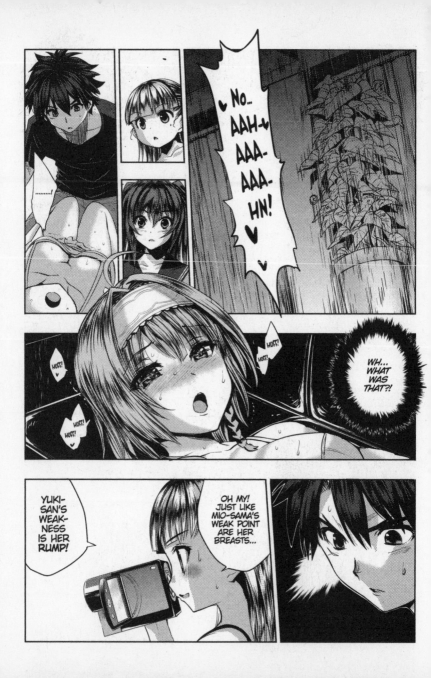

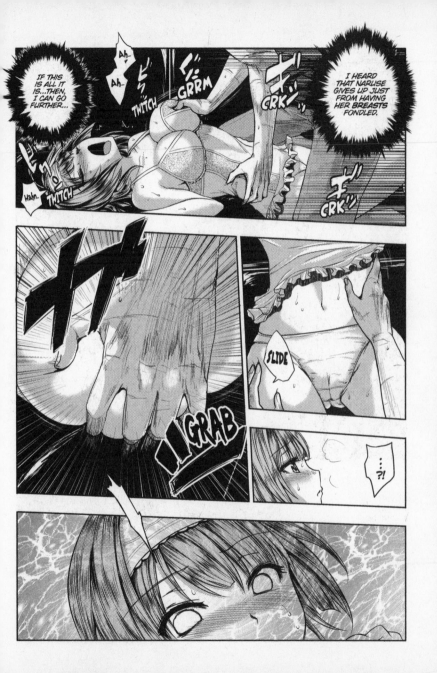

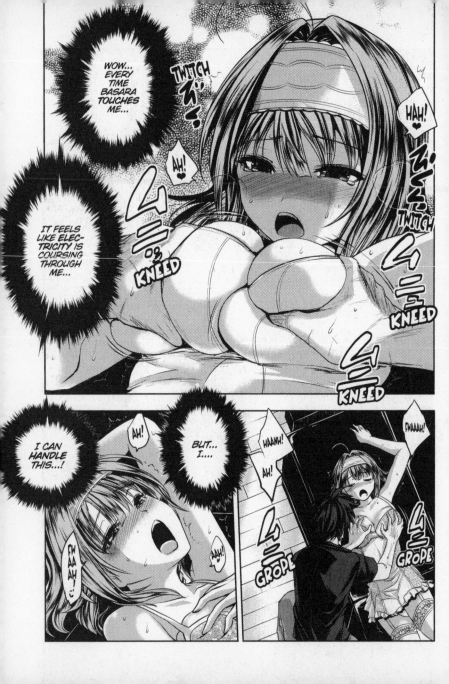

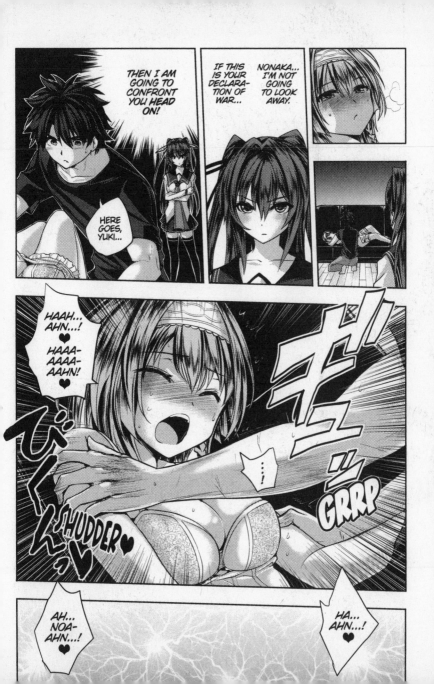

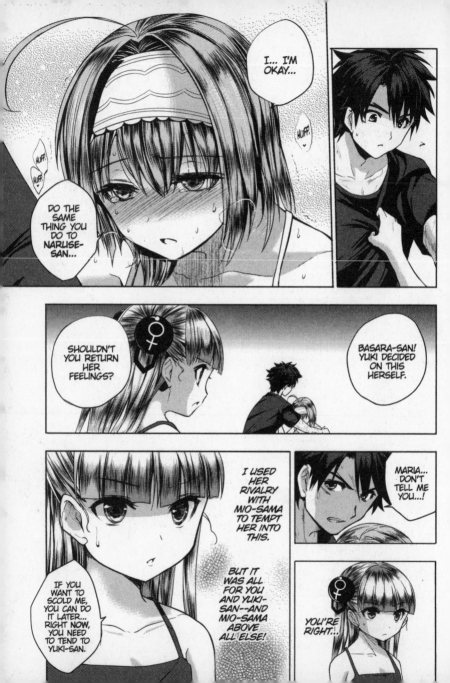

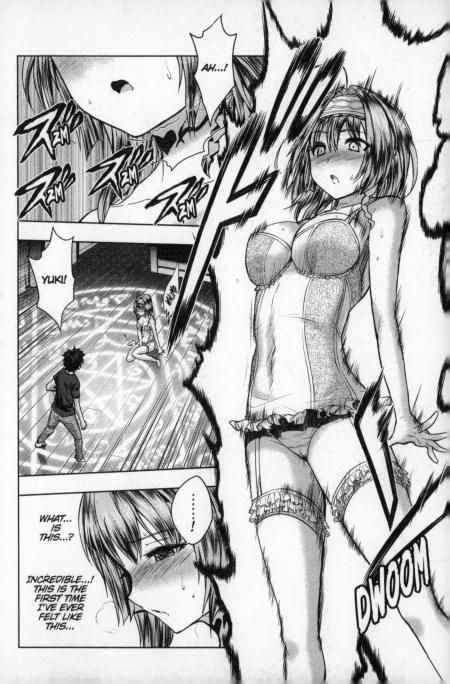

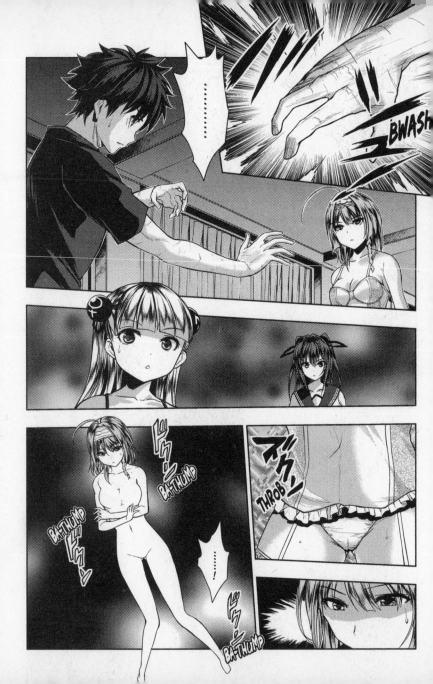

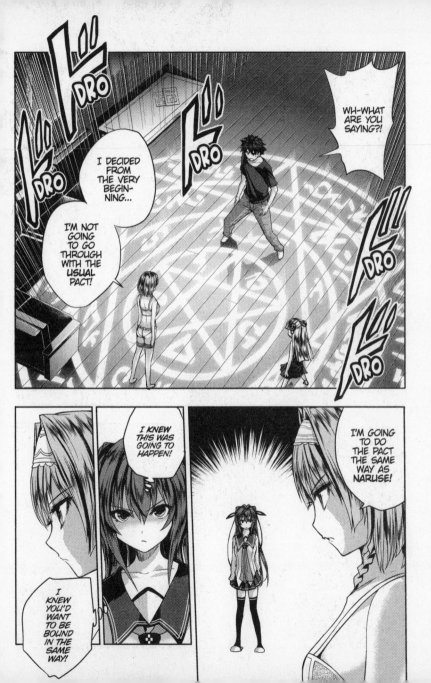

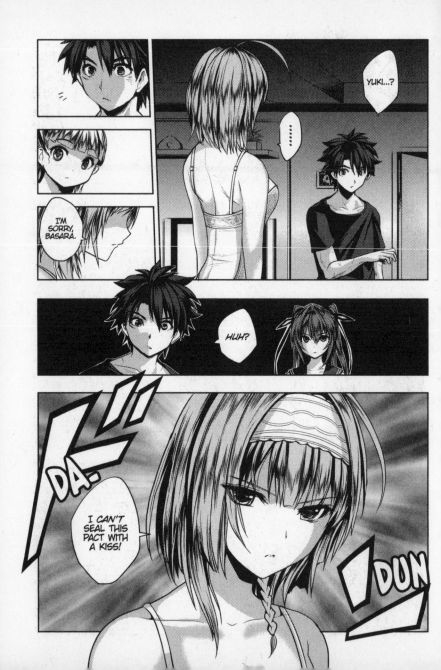

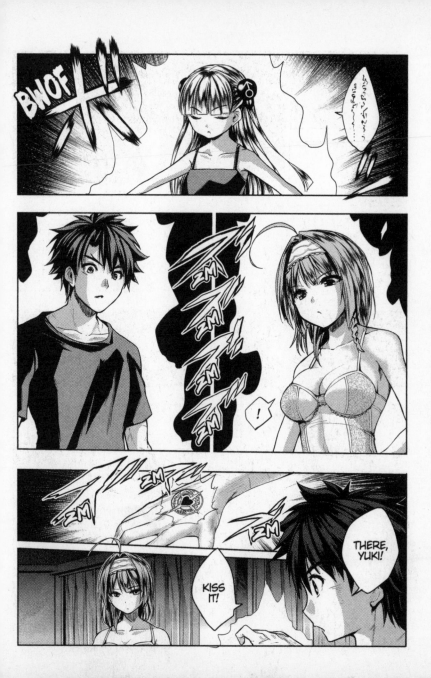

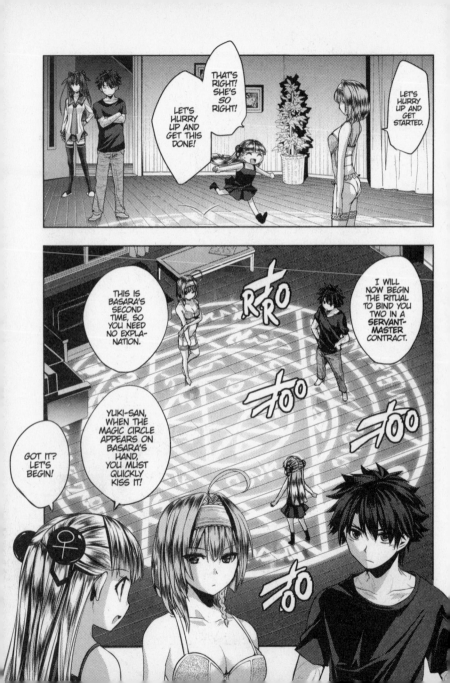

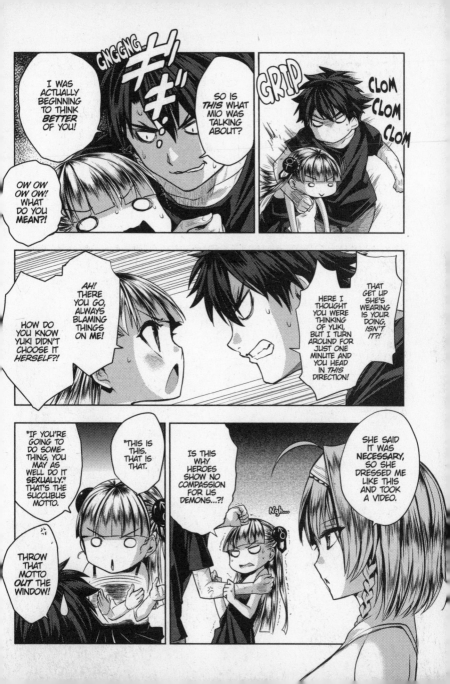

GNGGNG...

#! #"

GRIP

CLOM CLOM CLOM

I WAS ACTUALLY BEGINNING TO THINK *BETTER* OF YOU!

SO IS *THIS* WHAT MIO WAS TALKING ABOUT?

OW OW OW OW! WHAT DO YOU MEAN?!

HOW DO YOU KNOW YUKI DIDN'T CHOOSE IT *HERSELF?!*

AH! THERE YOU GO, ALWAYS BLAMING THINGS ON ME!

HERE I THOUGHT YOU WERE THINKING OF YUKI, BUT I TURN AROUND FOR JUST ONE MINUTE AND YOU HEAD IN *THIS* DIRECTION!

THAT GET UP SHE'S WEARING IS YOUR DOING, *ISN'T* IT?!

"IF YOU'RE GOING TO DO SOME-THING, YOU MAY AS WELL DO IT SEXUALLY." THAT'S THE SUCCUBUS MOTTO.

"THIS IS THIS. THAT IS THAT."

THROW THAT MOTTO *OUT* THE WINDOW!

IS THIS WHY HEROES SHOW NO COMPASSION FOR US DEMONS...?!

Ngh...

SHE SAID IT WAS NECESSARY, SO SHE DRESSED ME LIKE THIS AND TOOK A VIDEO.

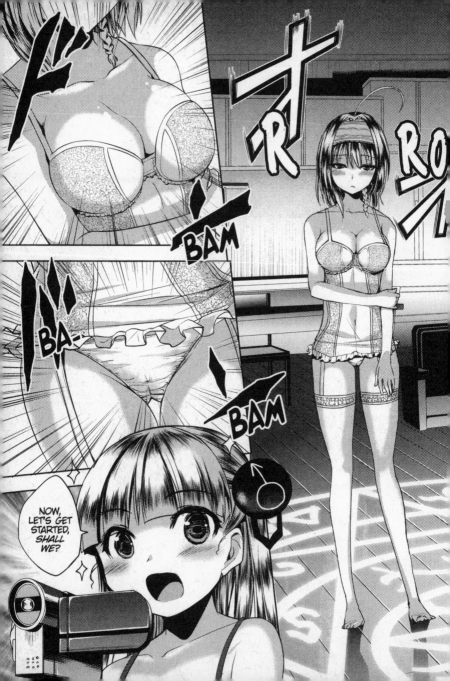

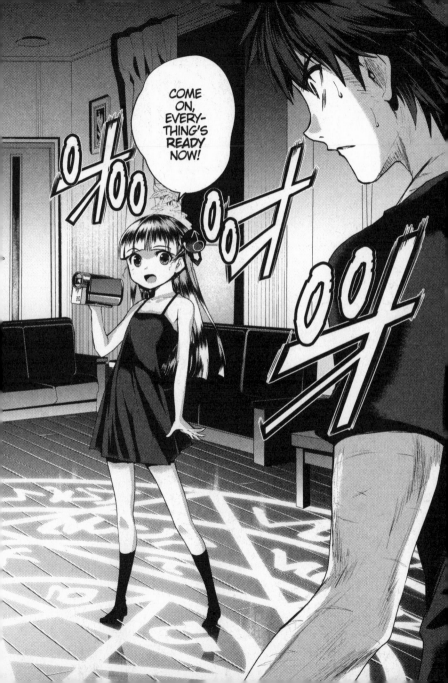

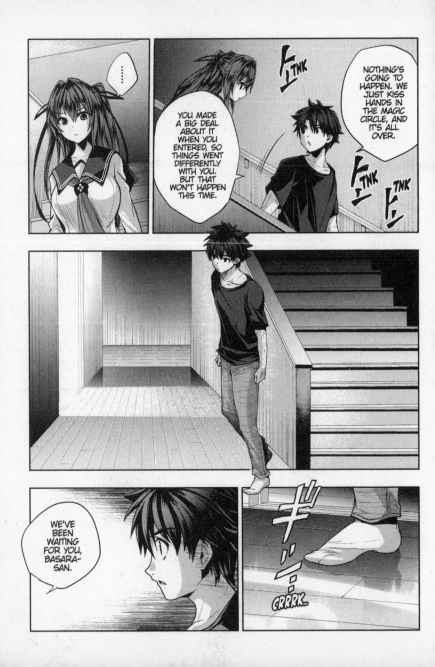

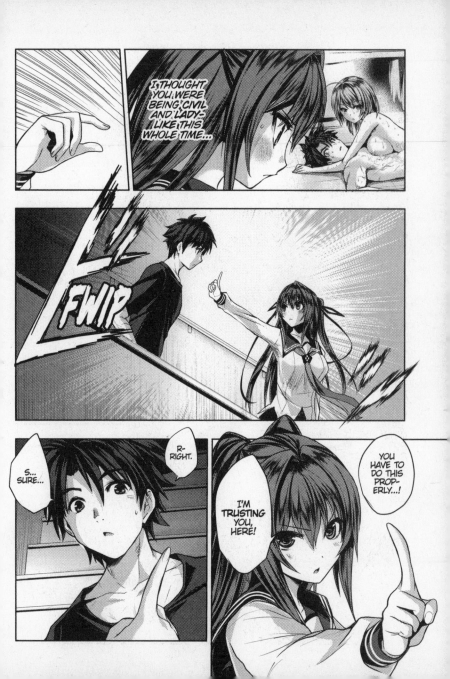

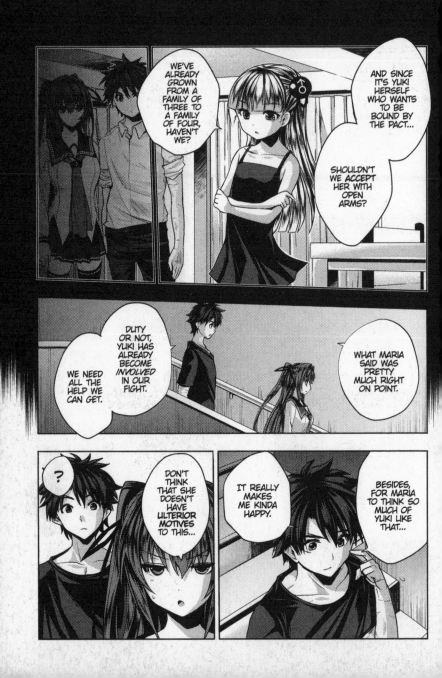

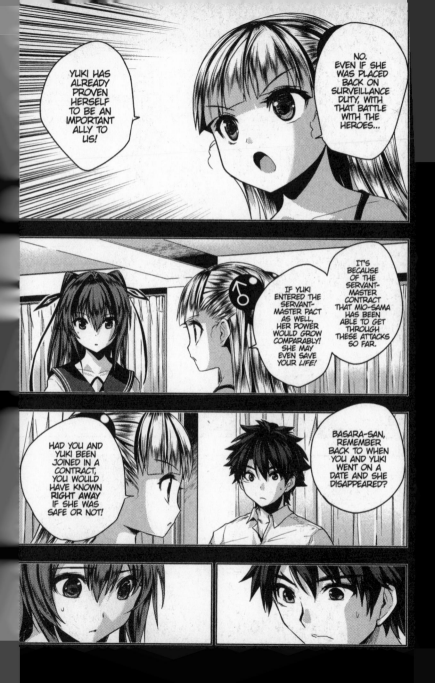

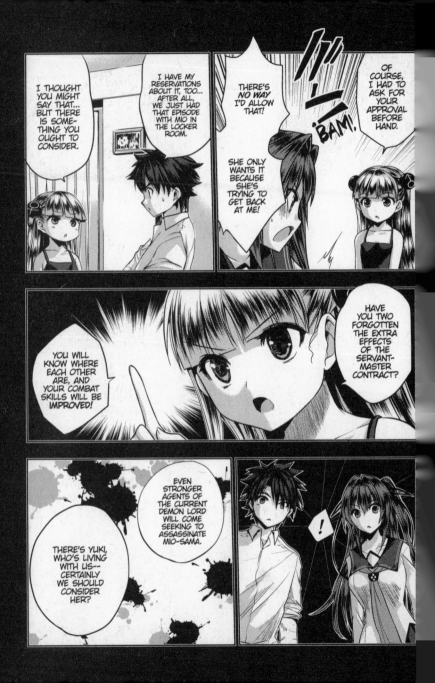

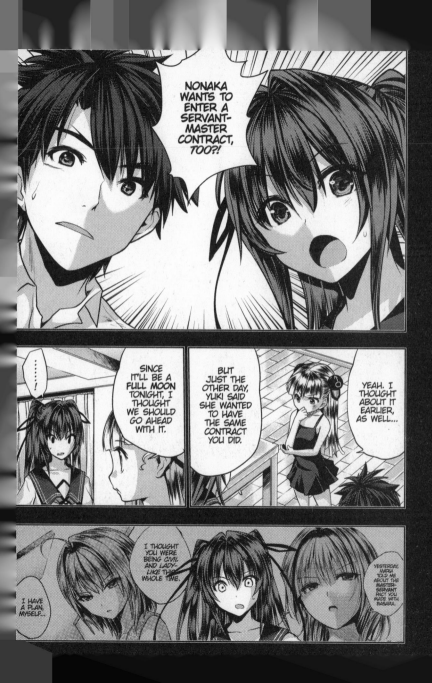

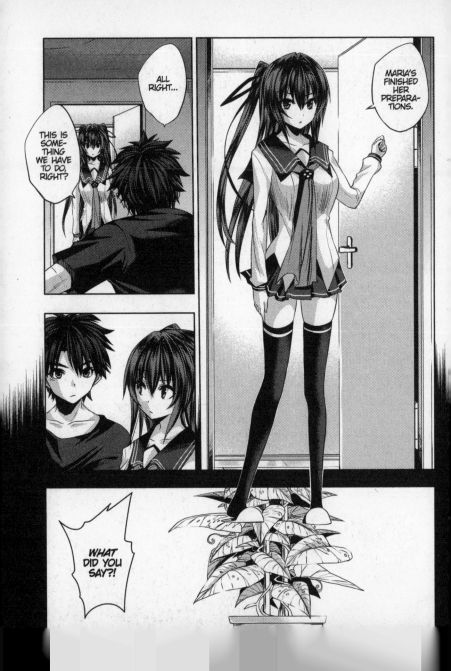

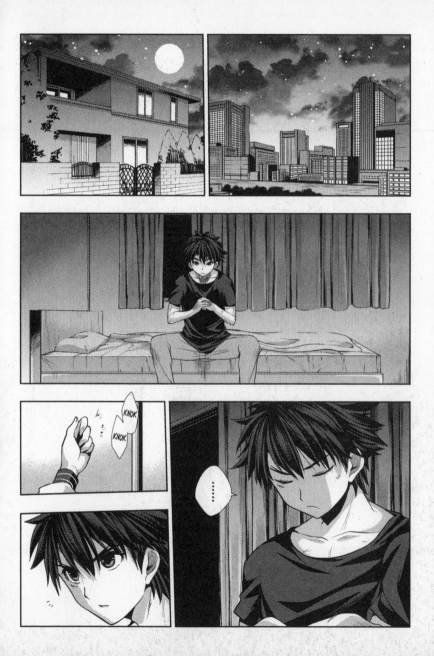

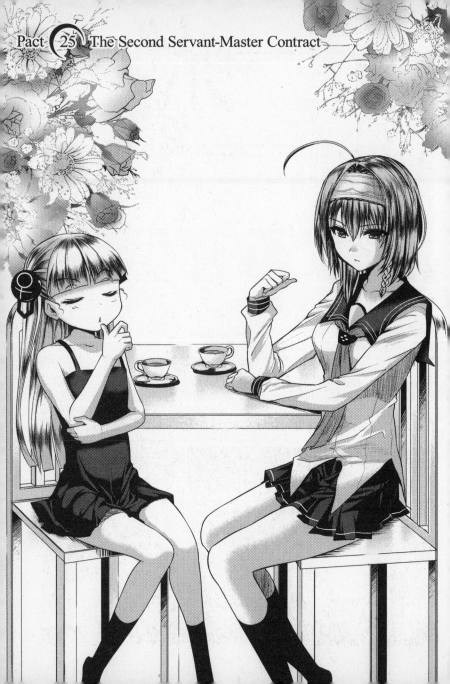

Pact 25 The Second Servant-Master Contract

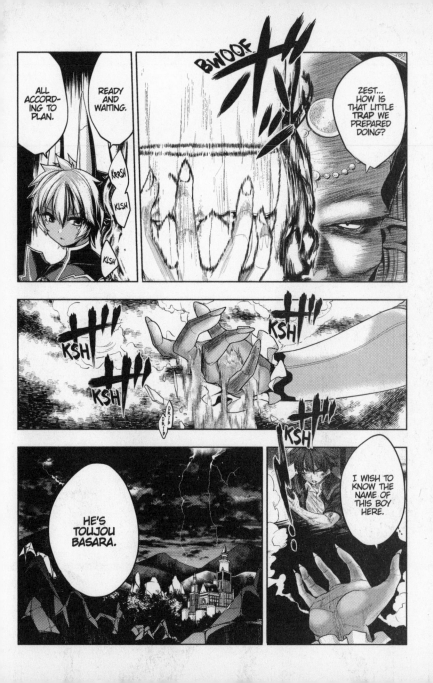

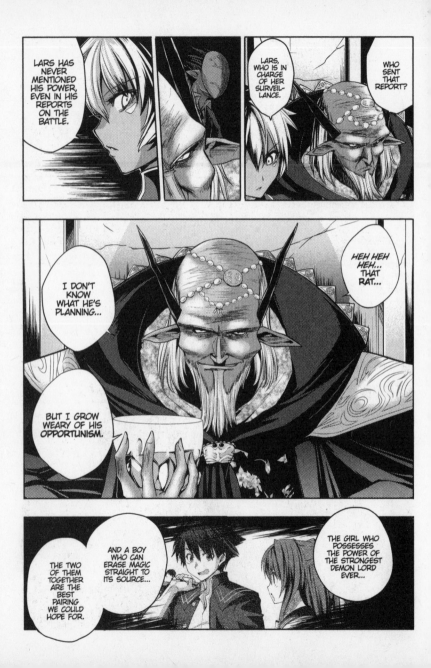

LARS HAS NEVER MENTIONED HIS POWER, EVEN IN HIS REPORTS ON THE BATTLE.

LARS, WHO IS IN CHARGE OF HER SURVEILLANCE.

WHO SENT THAT REPORT?

HEH HEH HEH... THAT RAT...

I DON'T KNOW WHAT HE'S PLANNING...

BUT I GROW WEARY OF HIS OPPORTUNISM.

THE GIRL WHO POSSESSES THE POWER OF THE STRONGEST DEMON LORD EVER...

AND A BOY WHO CAN ERASE MAGIC STRAIGHT TO ITS SOURCE...

THE TWO OF THEM TOGETHER ARE THE BEST PAIRING WE COULD HOPE FOR.

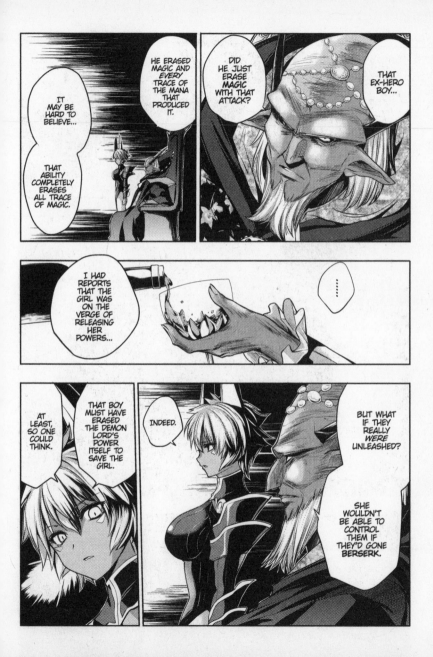

IT MAY BE HARD TO BELIEVE...

THAT ABILITY COMPLETELY ERASES ALL TRACE OF MAGIC.

HE ERASED MAGIC AND *EVERY* TRACE OF THE MANA THAT PRODUCED IT.

DID HE JUST ERASE MAGIC WITH THAT ATTACK?

THAT EX-HERO BOY...

I HAD REPORTS THAT THE GIRL WAS ON THE VERGE OF RELEASING HER POWERS...

.....

AT LEAST, SO ONE COULD THINK.

THAT BOY MUST HAVE ERASED THE DEMON LORD'S POWER ITSELF TO SAVE THE GIRL.

INDEED.

BUT WHAT IF THEY REALLY *WERE* UNLEASHED?

SHE WOULDN'T BE ABLE TO CONTROL THEM IF THEY'D GONE BERSERK.

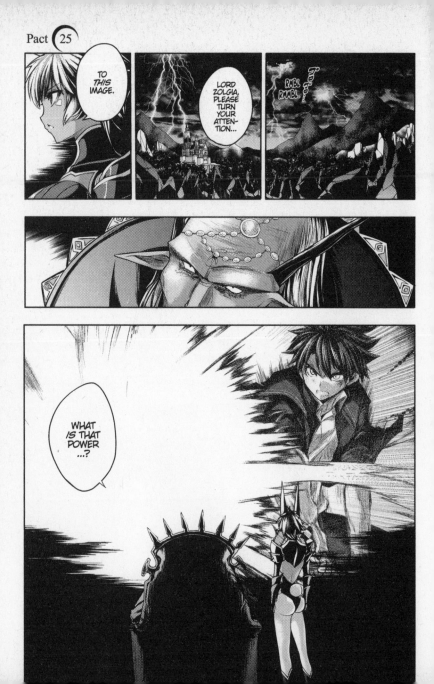

The Testament of
Sister New Devil

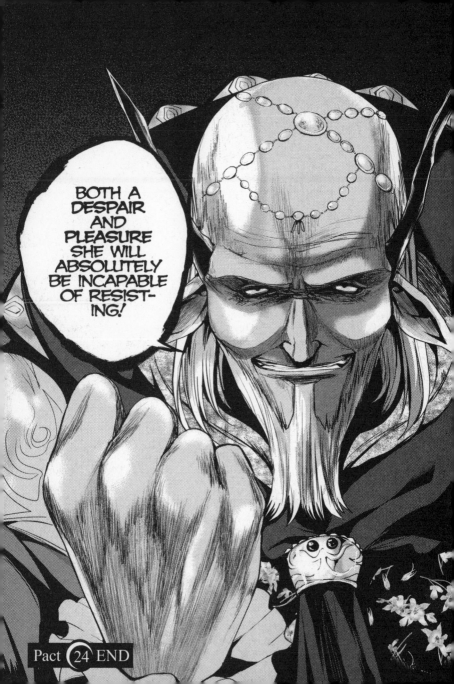

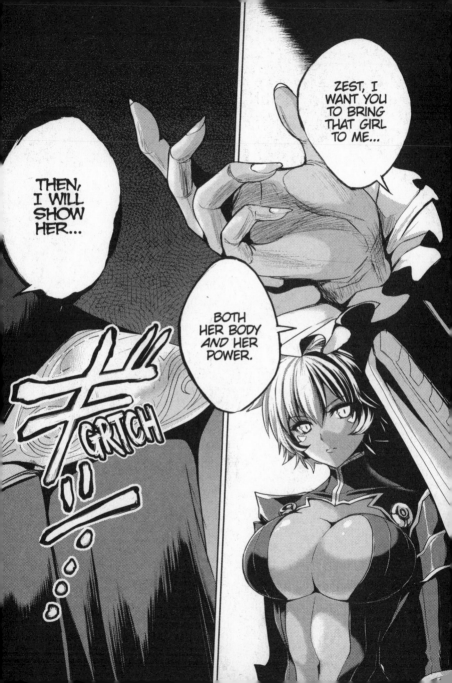

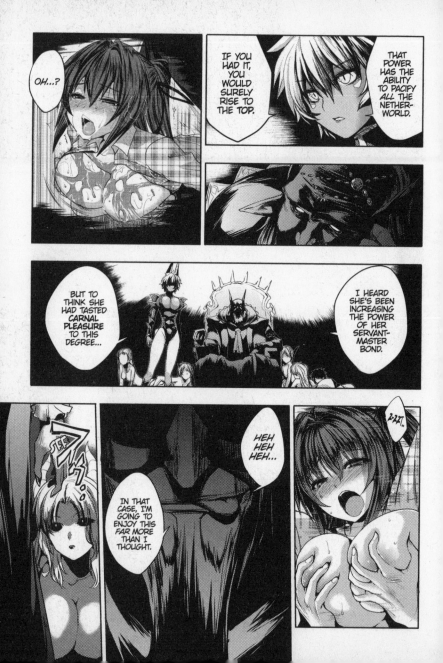

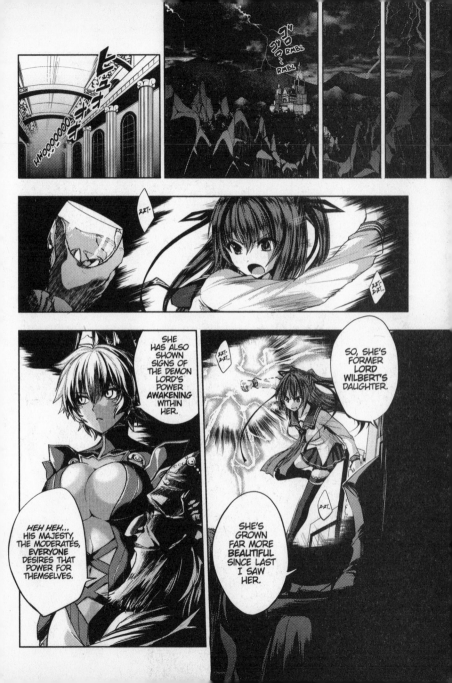

SHE HAS ALSO SHOWN SIGNS OF THE DEMON LORD'S POWER AWAKENING WITHIN HER.

SO, SHE'S FORMER LORD WILBERT'S DAUGHTER.

HEH HEH... HIS MAJESTY, THE MODERATES, EVERYONE DESIRES THAT POWER FOR THEMSELVES.

SHE'S GROWN FAR MORE BEAUTIFUL SINCE LAST I SAW HER.

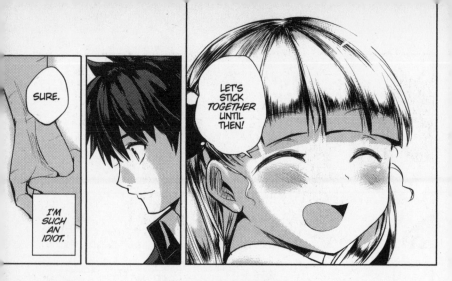

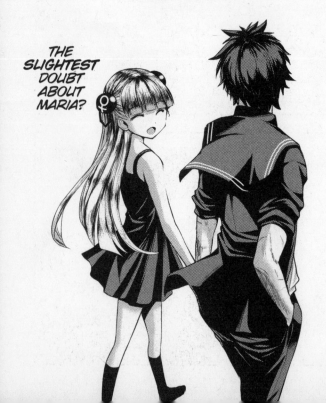

THE SLIGHTEST DOUBT ABOUT MARIA?

HOW COULD I HAVE...

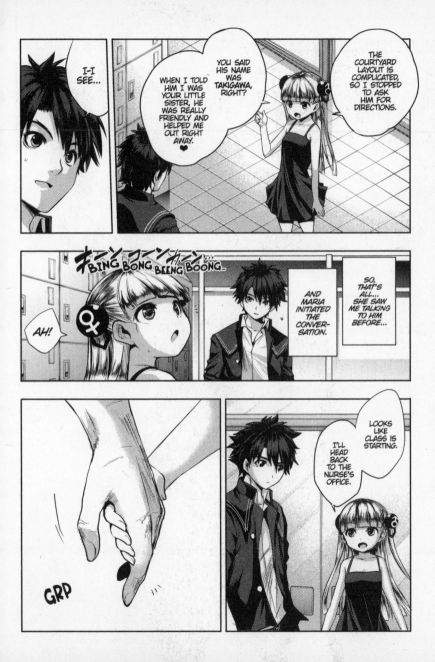

I-I SEE...

WHEN I TOLD HIM I WAS YOUR LITTLE SISTER, HE WAS REALLY FRIENDLY AND HELPED ME OUT RIGHT AWAY.

YOU SAID HIS NAME WAS TAKIGAWA, RIGHT?

THE COURTYARD LAYOUT IS COMPLICATED, SO I STOPPED TO ASK HIM FOR DIRECTIONS.

BING BONG BEENG BOONG

AH!

AND MARIA INITIATED THE CONVER-SATION.

SO, THAT'S ALL... SHE SAW ME TALKING TO HIM BEFORE...

GRP

I'LL HEAD BACK TO THE NURSE'S OFFICE.

LOOKS LIKE CLASS IS STARTING.

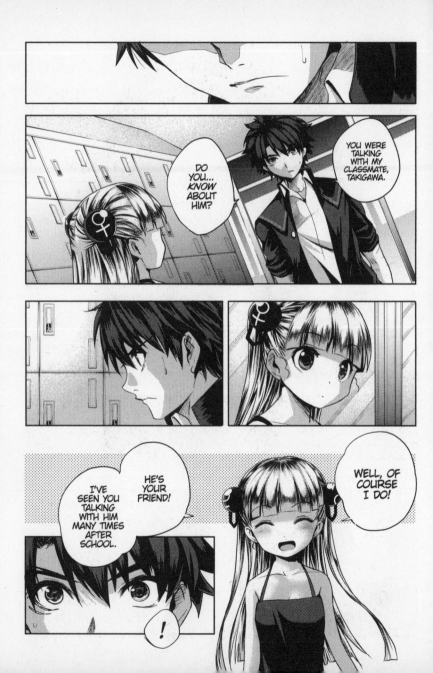

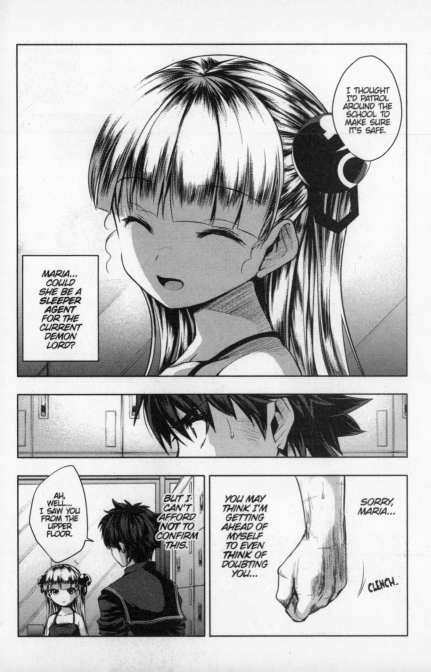

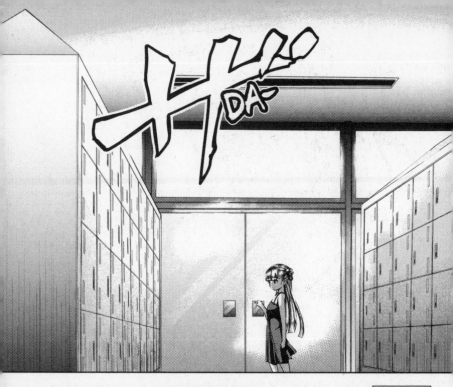

DA-

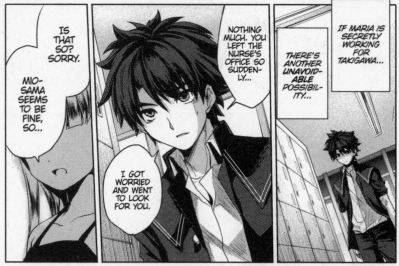

IS THAT SO? SORRY.

MIO-SAMA SEEMS TO BE FINE, SO...

NOTHING MUCH. YOU LEFT THE NURSE'S OFFICE SO SUDDEN-LY...

I GOT WORRIED AND WENT TO LOOK FOR YOU.

THERE'S ANOTHER UNAVOID-ABLE POSSIBIL-ITY...

IF MARIA IS SECRETLY WORKING FOR TAKIGAWA...

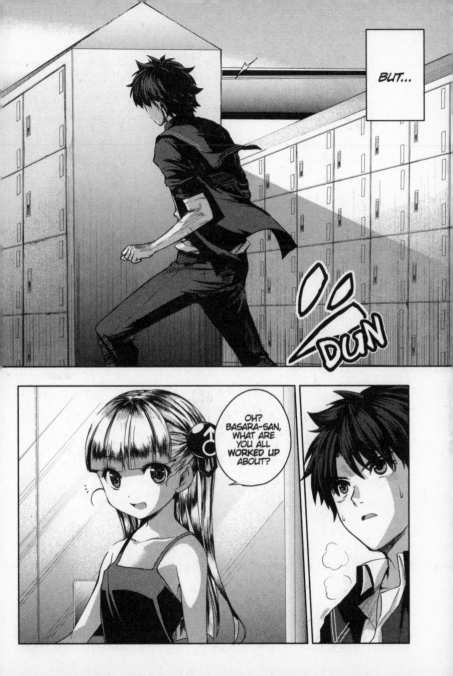

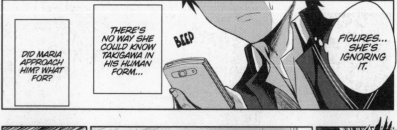

DID MARIA APPROACH HIM? WHAT FOR?

THERE'S NO WAY SHE COULD KNOW TAKIGAWA IN HIS HUMAN FORM...

BEEP

FIGURES... SHE'S IGNORING IT.

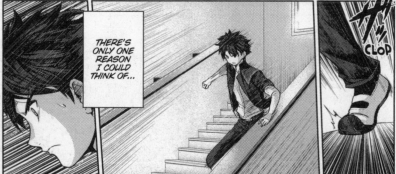

THERE'S ONLY ONE REASON I COULD THINK OF...

CLOP

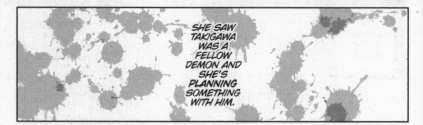

SHE SAW TAKIGAWA WAS A FELLOW DEMON AND SHE'S PLANNING SOMETHING WITH HIM.

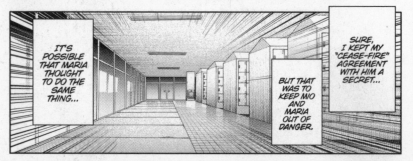

IT'S POSSIBLE THAT MARIA THOUGHT TO DO THE SAME THING...

BUT THAT WAS TO KEEP MIO AND MARIA OUT OF DANGER.

SURE, I KEPT MY "CEASE-FIRE" AGREEMENT WITH HIM A SECRET...

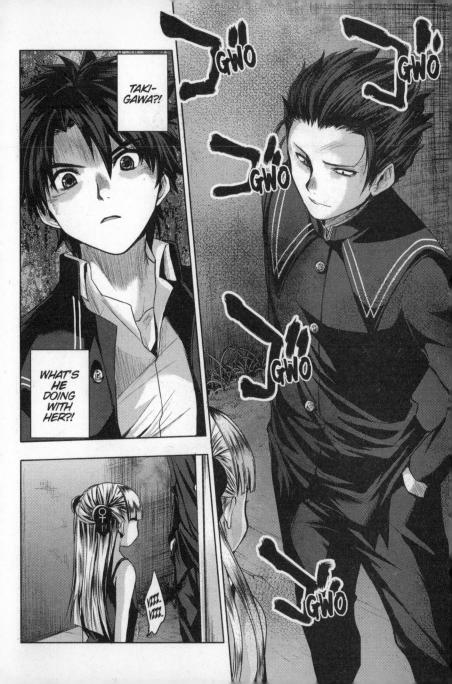

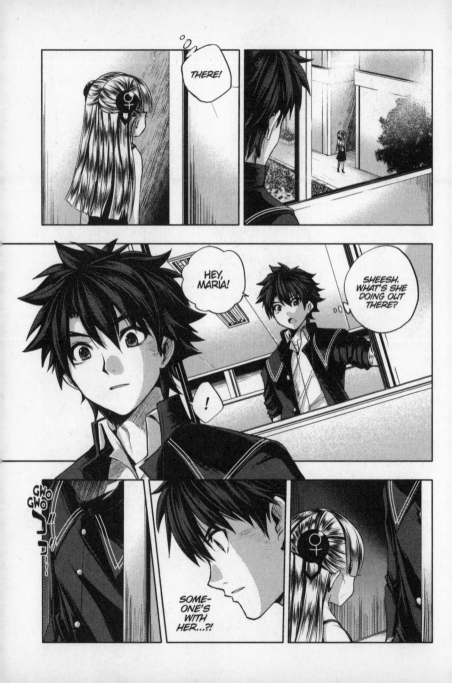

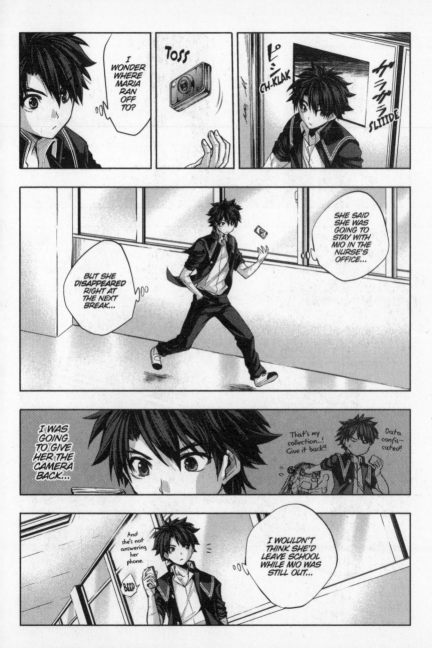

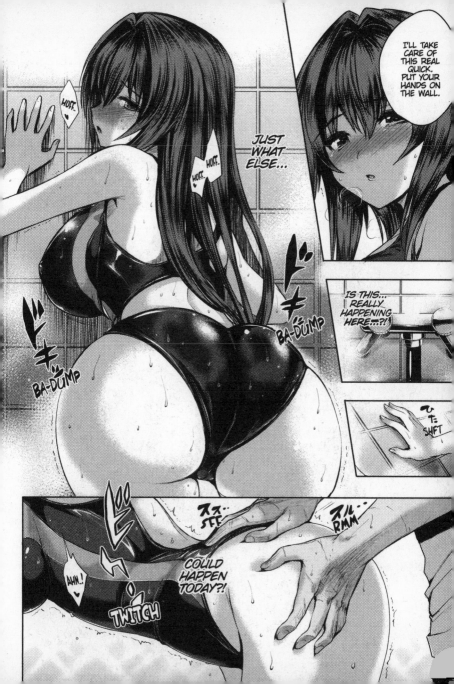

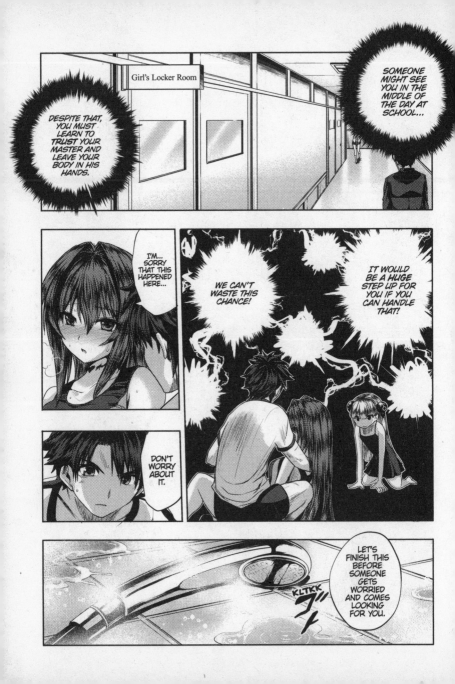

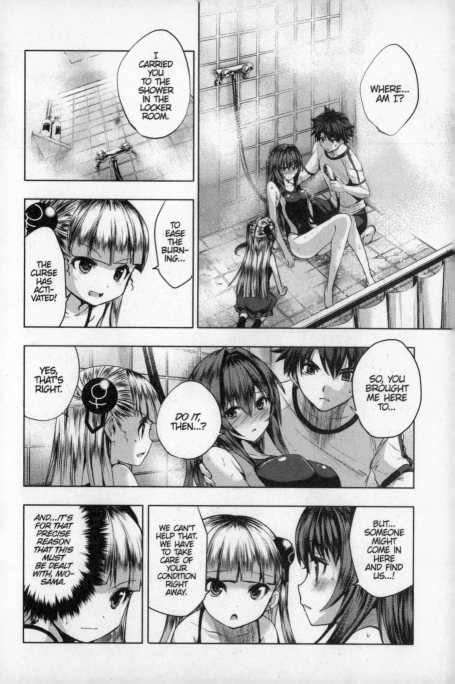

I CARRIED YOU TO THE SHOWER IN THE LOCKER ROOM.

WHERE... AM I?

TO EASE THE BURNING...

THE CURSE HAS ACTIVATED!

YES, THAT'S RIGHT.

DO IT, THEN...?

SO, YOU BROUGHT ME HERE TO...

AND...IT'S FOR THAT PRECISE REASON THAT THIS MUST BE DEALT WITH, NIO-SAMA.

WE CAN'T HELP THAT. WE HAVE TO TAKE CARE OF YOUR CONDITION RIGHT AWAY.

BUT... SOMEONE MIGHT COME IN HERE AND FIND US...!

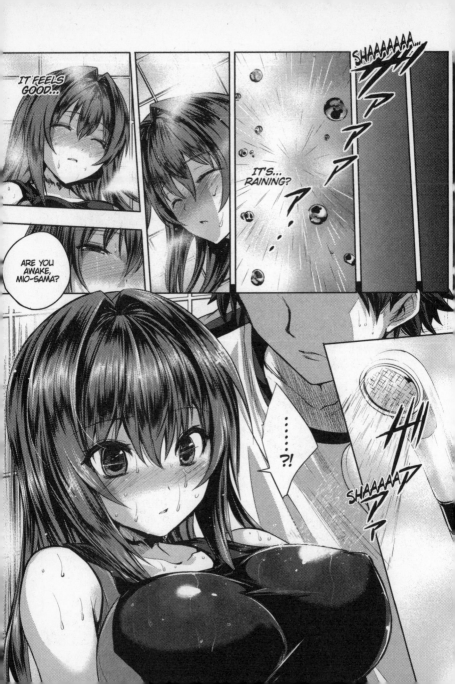

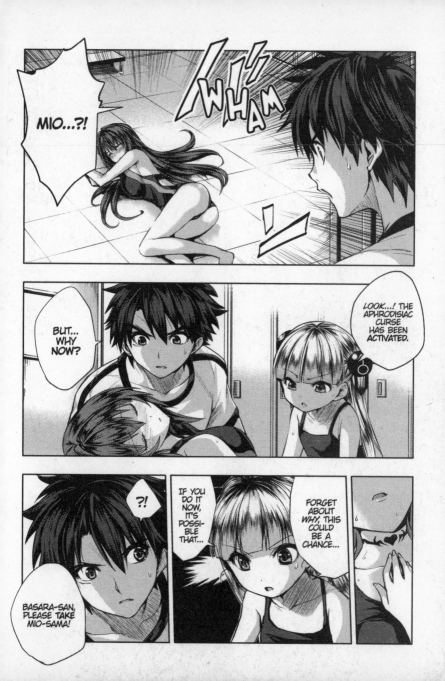

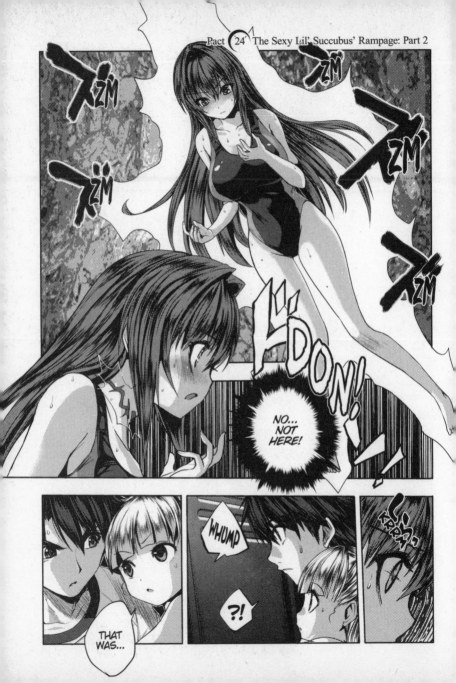

The Testament of
Sister New Devil

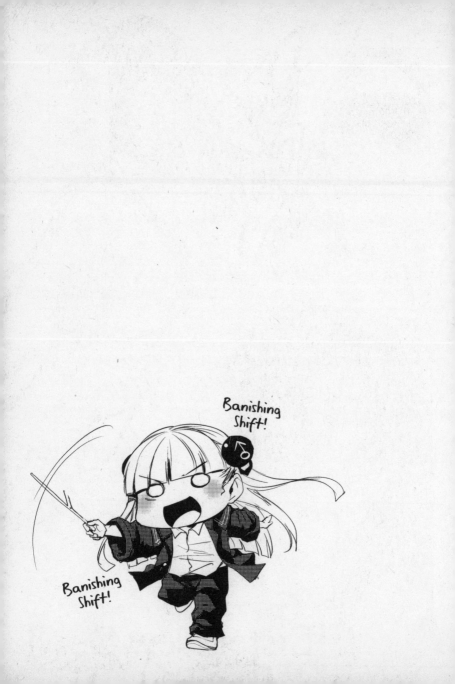

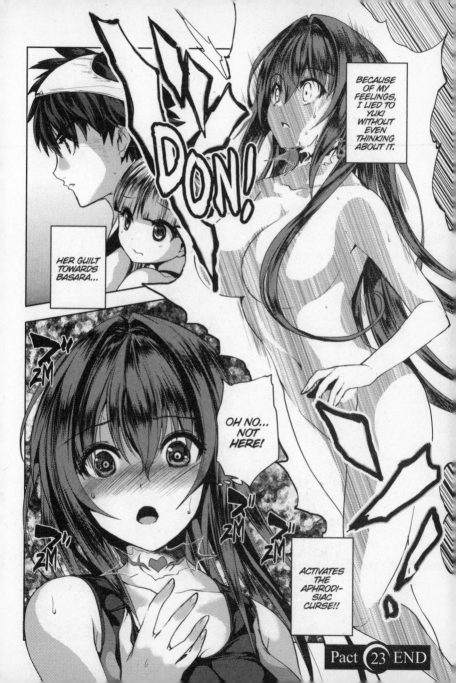

BECAUSE OF MY FEELINGS, I LIED TO YUKI WITHOUT EVEN THINKING ABOUT IT.

DON!

HER GUILT TOWARDS BASARA...

OH NO... NOT HERE!

ACTIVATES THE APHRODI-SIAC CURSE!!

Pact 23 END

I JUST LIED WITHOUT EVEN THINKING. I DIDN'T EVEN HAVE TO HIDE IT FROM NONAKA, WHO ALREADY KNOWS THE SITUATION...

I'M NOT EVEN THAT MAD, REALLY.

IT'S FINE.

JUST BETWEEN US.

I WANTED IT TO BE A PROBLEM...

I LIED...

I WAS JEALOUS...

ZMM...

I WANTED HIM TO MYSELF...

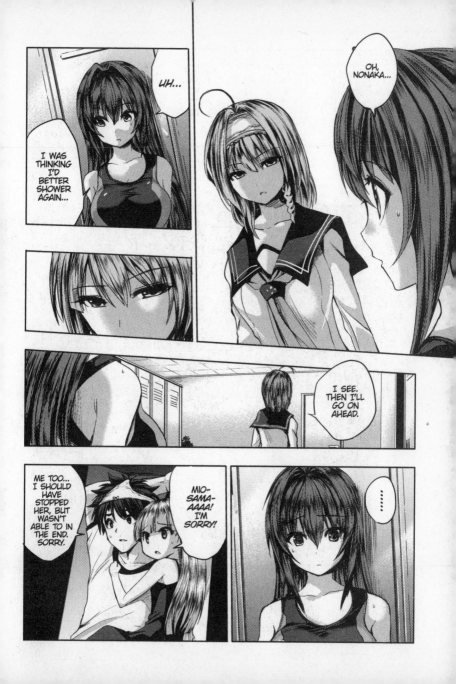

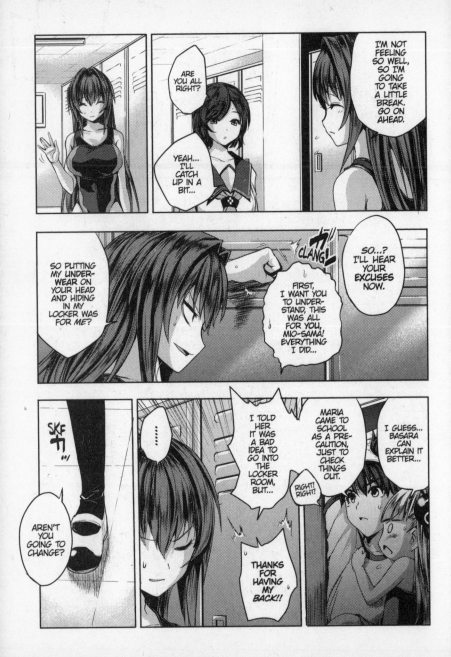

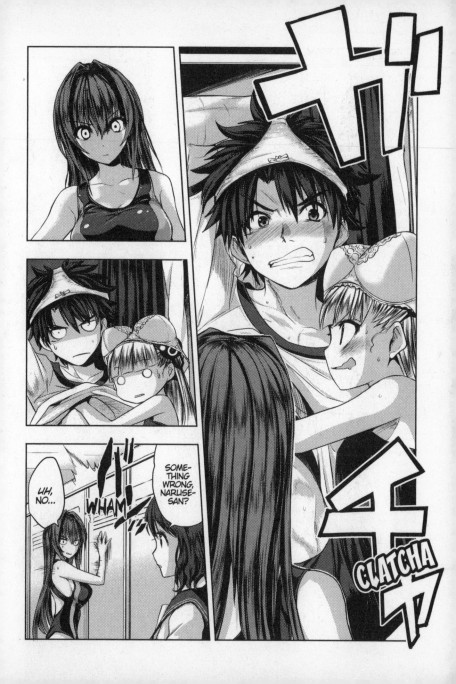

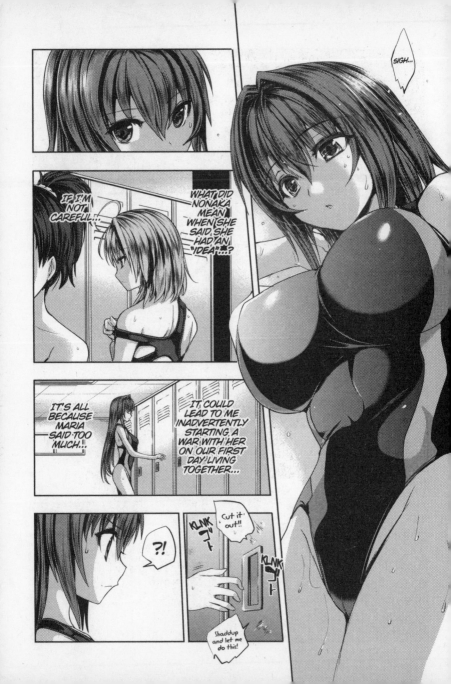

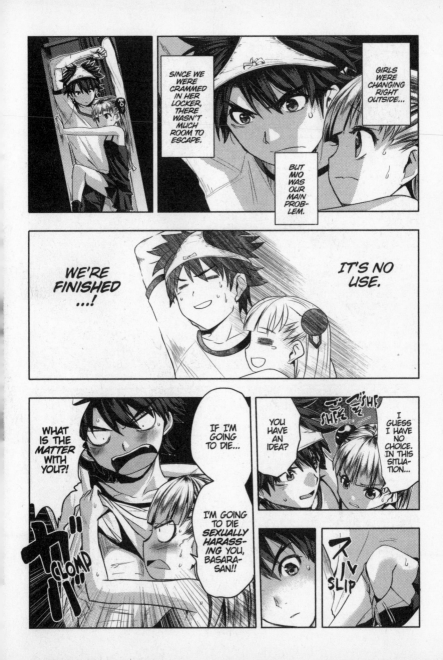

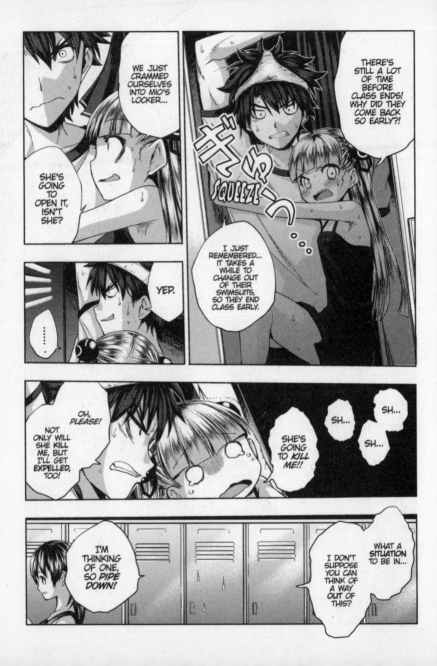

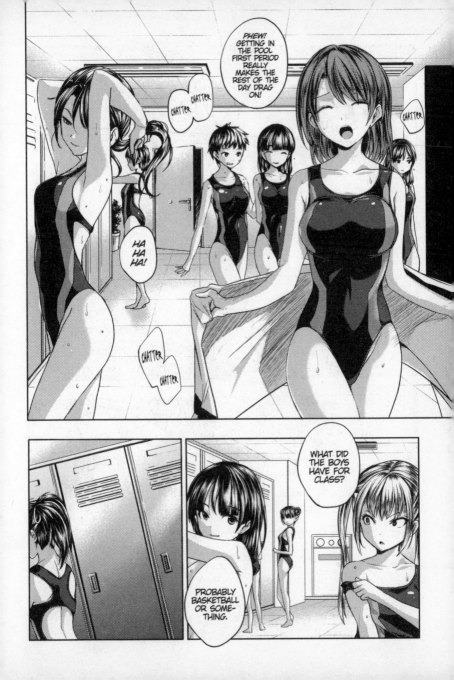

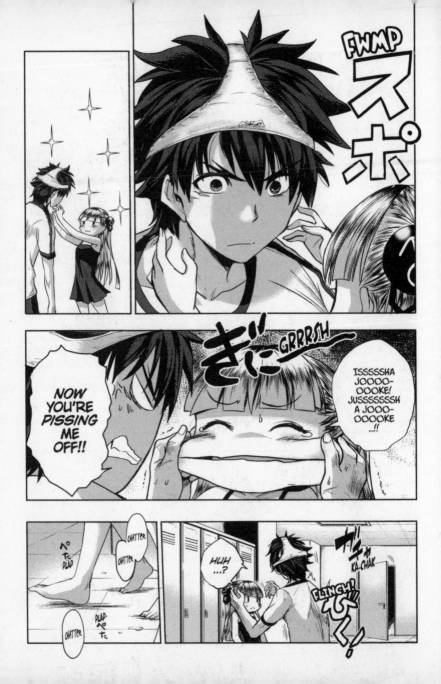

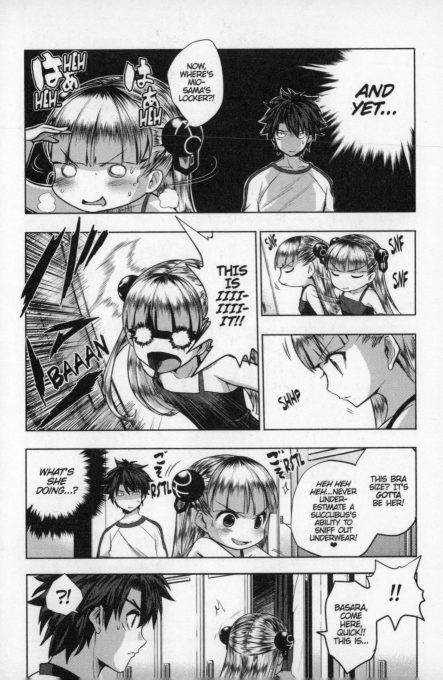

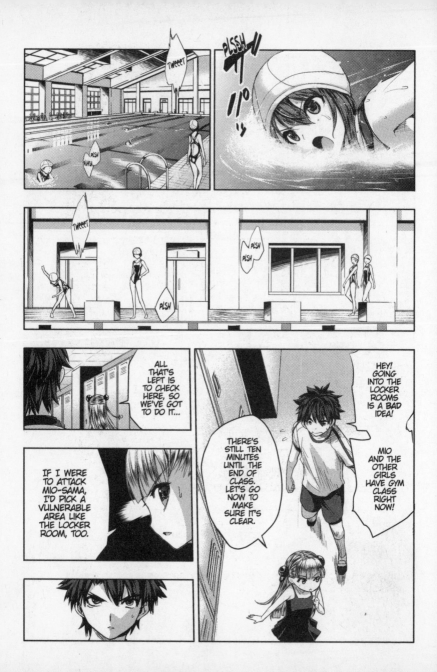

TWEEET

PLSSH

PLSH
PLSSH

TWEEET

PLSH
PLSH

PLSH

ALL THAT'S LEFT IS TO CHECK HERE, SO WE'VE GOT TO DO IT...

IF I WERE TO ATTACK MIO-SAMA, I'D PICK A VULNERABLE AREA LIKE THE LOCKER ROOM, TOO.

THERE'S STILL TEN MINUTES UNTIL THE END OF CLASS. LET'S GO NOW TO MAKE SURE IT'S CLEAR.

HEY! GOING INTO THE LOCKER ROOMS IS A BAD IDEA!

MIO AND THE OTHER GIRLS HAVE GYM CLASS RIGHT NOW!

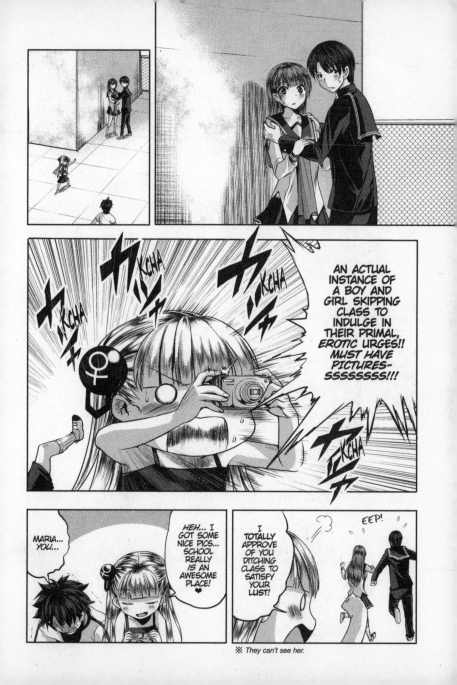

AN ACTUAL INSTANCE OF A BOY AND GIRL SKIPPING CLASS TO INDULGE IN THEIR PRIMAL, *EROTIC* URGES!! MUST HAVE PICTURES-SSSSSSSSS!!!

KCHA KCHA KCHA KCHA KCHA

MARIA... YOU...

HEH... I GOT SOME NICE PICS... SCHOOL REALLY *IS* AN AWESOME PLACE!

I TOTALLY APPROVE OF YOU DITCHING CLASS TO SATISFY YOUR LUST!

EEP!

※ They can't see her.

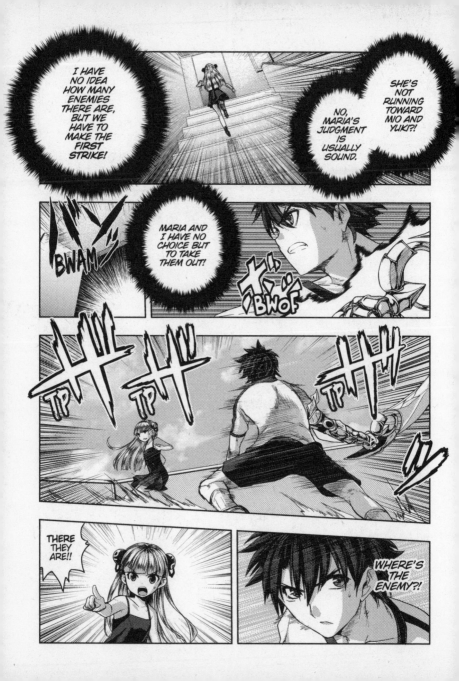

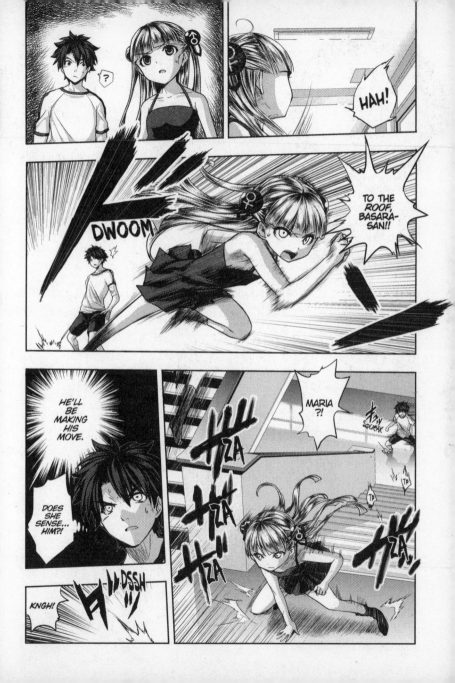

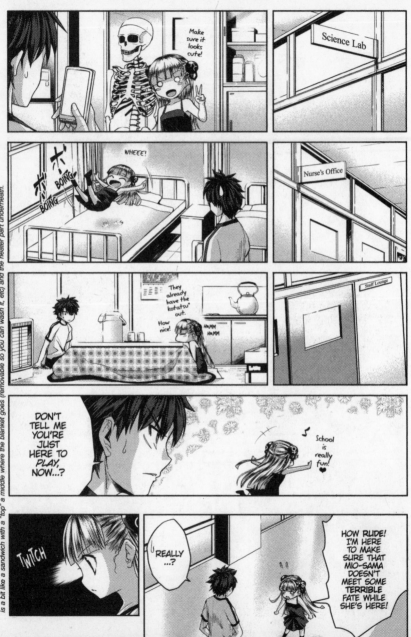

Make sure it looks cute!

Science Lab

WHEEE!

BOING
BOING
BOING

Nurse's Office

They already have the kotatsu* out.

How nice!

HMMM HMMM

Staff Lounge

DON'T TELL ME YOU'RE JUST HERE TO *PLAY*, NOW...?

School is really fun! ♥

*Kotatsu - a low table with a blanket and a heater underneath. Used especially in winter to heat your legs as you sit under it. The structure is a bit like a sandwich with a "top" a middle where the blanket goes (removable so you can wash it, etc) and the heater part underneath.

TWITCH

REALLY ...?

HOW RUDE! I'M HERE TO MAKE SURE THAT MIO-SAMA DOESN'T MEET SOME TERRIBLE FATE WHILE SHE'S HERE!

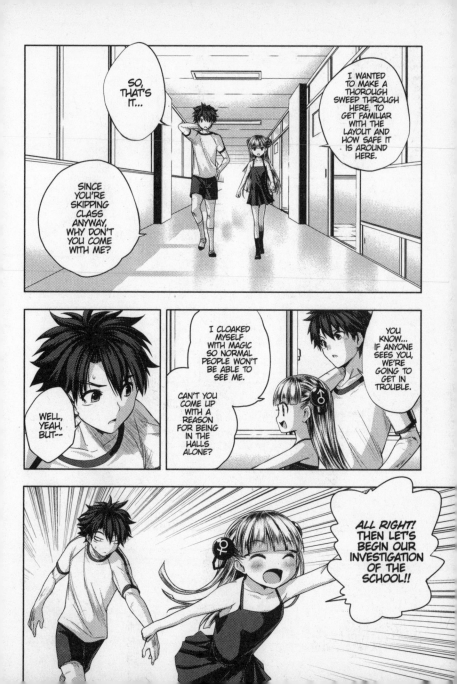

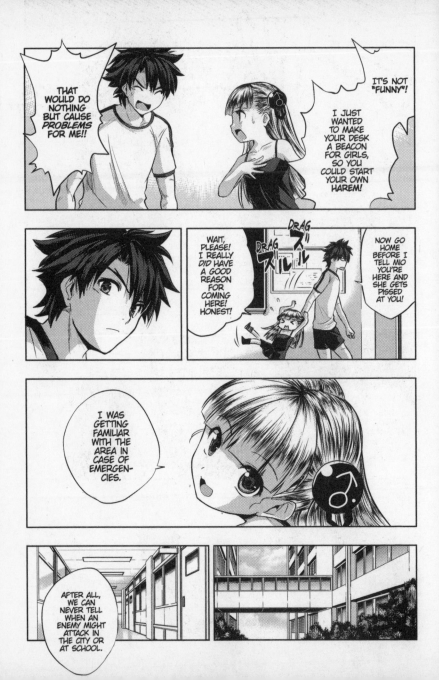

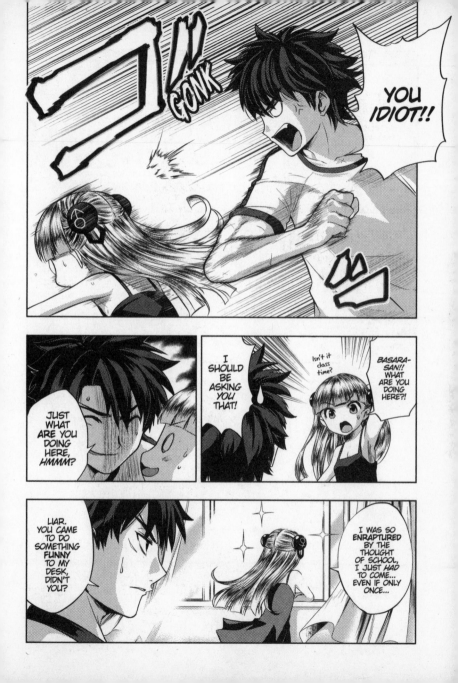

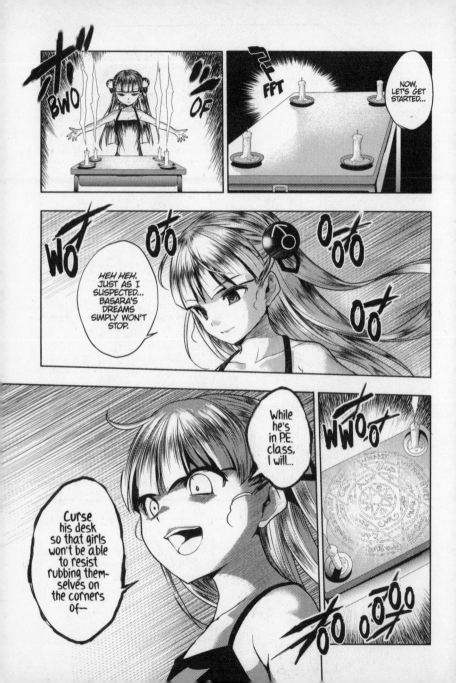

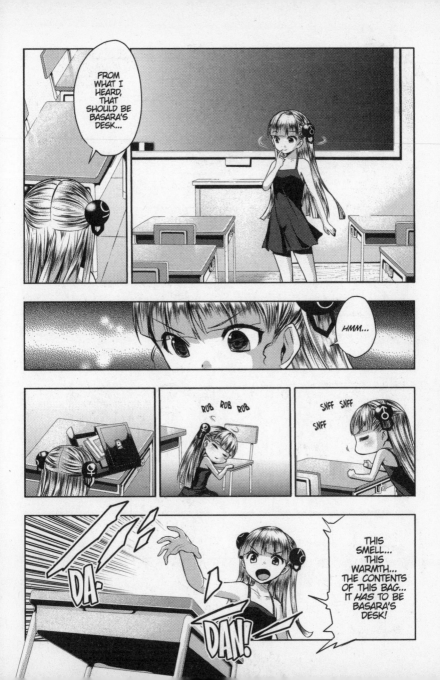

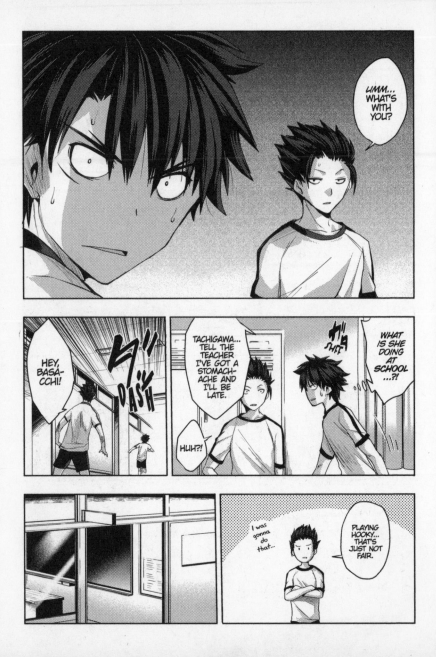

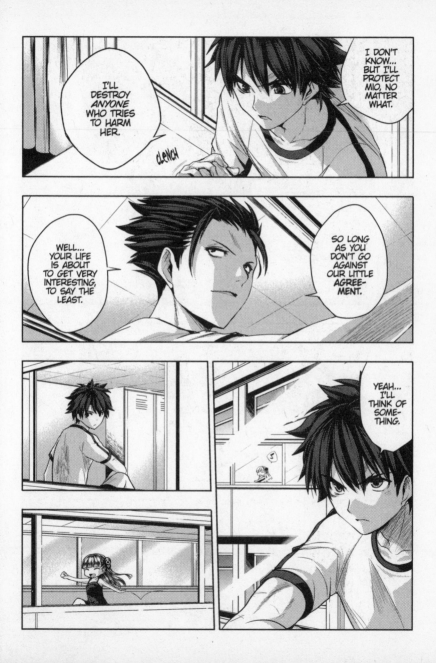

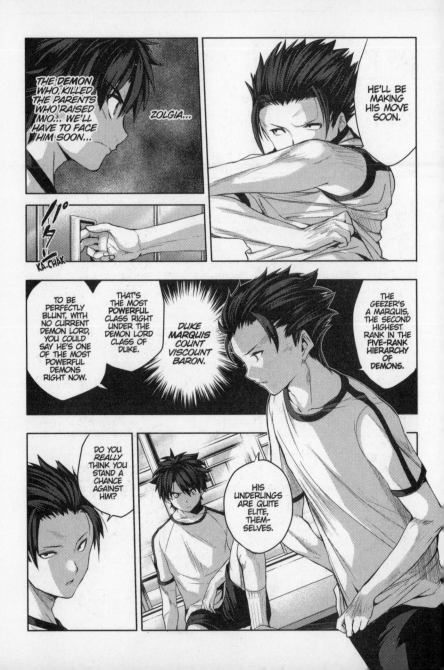

THE DEMON WHO KILLED THE PARENTS WHO RAISED MIO... WE'LL HAVE TO FACE HIM SOON...

ZOLGIA...

HE'LL BE MAKING HIS MOVE SOON.

KA-CHAK

TO BE PERFECTLY BLUNT, WITH NO CURRENT DEMON LORD, YOU COULD SAY HE'S ONE OF THE MOST POWERFUL DEMONS RIGHT NOW.

THAT'S THE MOST POWERFUL CLASS RIGHT UNDER THE DEMON LORD CLASS OF DUKE.

DUKE MARQUIS COUNT VISCOUNT BARON.

THE GEEZER'S A MARQUIS, THE SECOND HIGHEST RANK IN THE FIVE-RANK HIERARCHY OF DEMONS.

DO YOU REALLY THINK YOU STAND A CHANCE AGAINST HIM?

HIS UNDERLINGS ARE QUITE ELITE, THEM- SELVES.

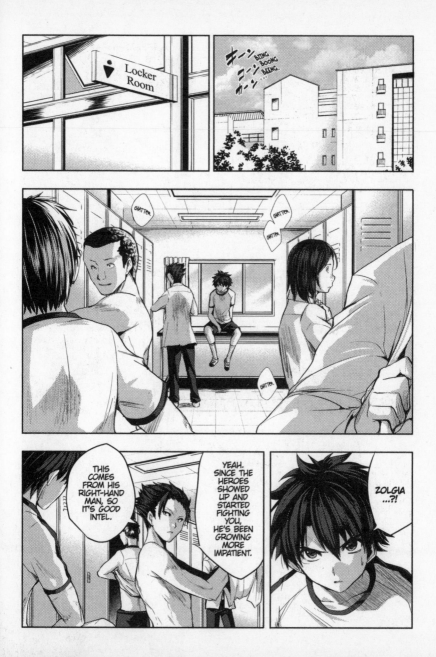

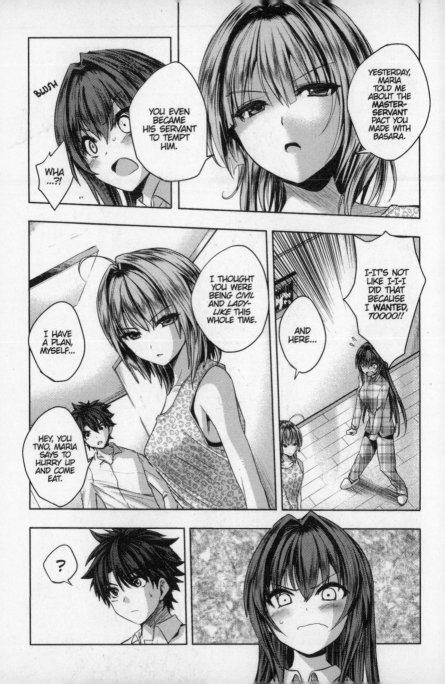

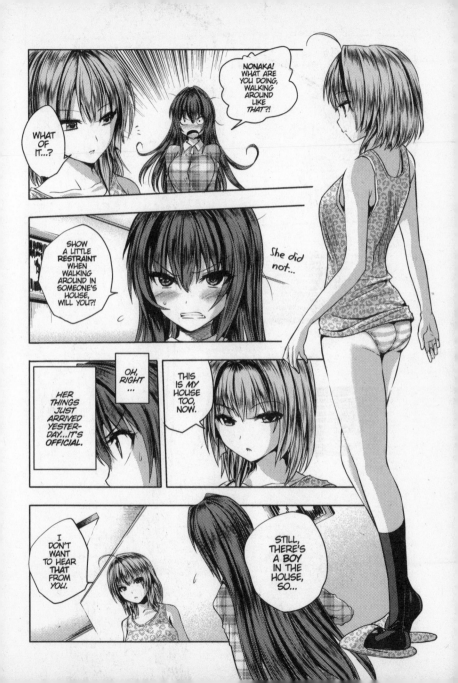

NONAKA! WHAT ARE YOU DOING, WALKING AROUND LIKE *THAT?!*

WHAT OF IT...?

SHOW A LITTLE RESTRAINT WHEN WALKING AROUND IN SOMEONE'S HOUSE, WILL YOU?!

She did not...

OH, RIGHT...

HER THINGS JUST ARRIVED YESTER- DAY...IT'S OFFICIAL.

THIS IS *MY* HOUSE TOO, NOW.

I DON'T WANT TO HEAR THAT FROM YOU.

STILL, THERE'S A BOY IN THE HOUSE, SO...

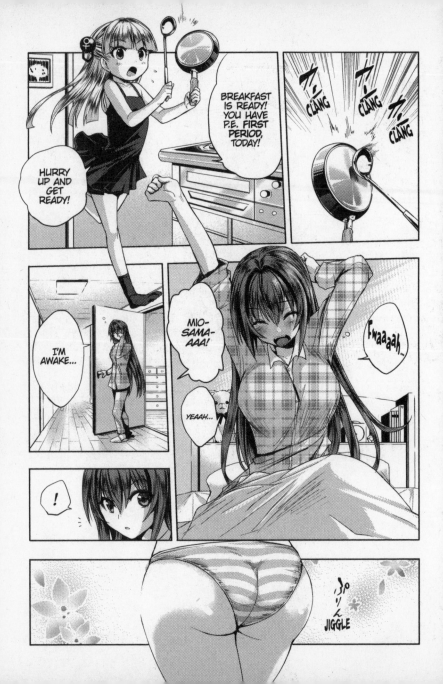

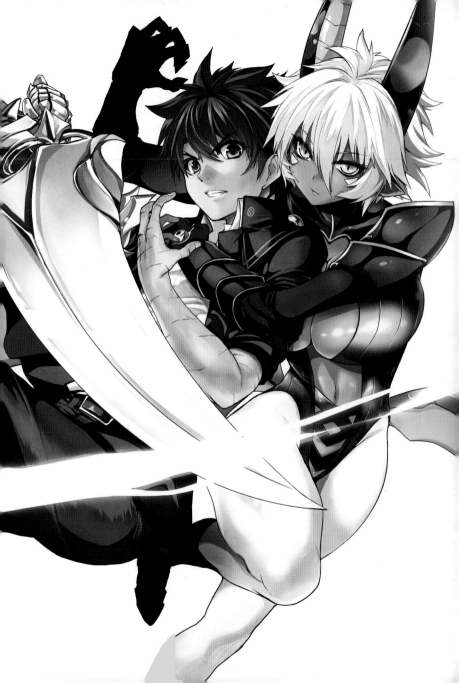

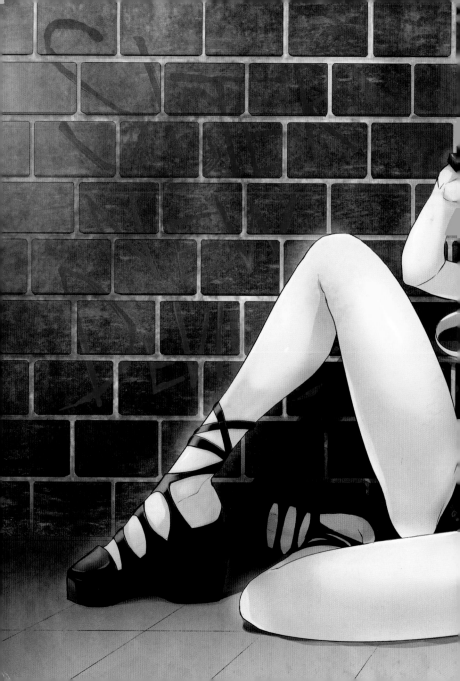

The Testament of 新妹魔王の契約者
Sister New Devil

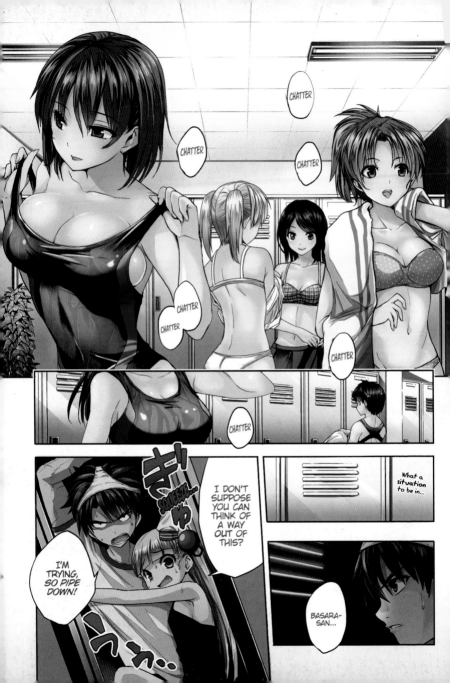

CHATTER

CHATTER

CHATTER

CHATTER

CHATTER

CHATTER

CHATTER

CHATTER

I DON'T SUPPOSE YOU CAN THINK OF A WAY OUT OF THIS?

I'M TRYING, SO PIPE DOWN!

What a situation to be in....

BASARA-SAN...